Found on the Alcan

Drue M. Scott

Found on the Alcan

Copyright © 2013 by **Drue M. Scott**

Printed in Canada
ISBN: 978-0-615-93695-6

This book was only made possible by the support of a number of great people: Jessica Contreras, Erika Wentworth, Samuel Smock, Becca Shevlin, Lauren Grant, and many others.

For it is through you that I found I am not alone.

Thank you.

Renee

Thank you!
I hope you
enjoy the book!

Warmest,

~Day 1~

"Smoke and mirrors, nothing more, a façade so perfectly made.
Daily living out these lies, the real me starts to fade."

~Leaving Home~

*E*arly morning sun filtered through my window as I lay staring at the corner of my empty room, looking into its simple white walls as though I were gazing off into an incalculable density of stars. I'd spent so many days readying myself for this moment that I couldn't believe I'd actually arrived at it. I was taking my last breaths as an Alaska resident before heading to the sunshine state and a new job. Alaska left me with many memories -- some happy, some sad -- but it was time now to take a leap of faith and make the drive to my new home in Orlando. I had never made such a big move on my own, such a grand re-envisioning of my daily life. Accepting a job in Florida and making the 5,000-mile drive alone -- using the maps, the tour books, figuring it all out as I went -- suddenly seemed a much larger task than I could possibly be capable of. I stopped staring at the corner, and with a muted sigh, refocused myself to the moment. Evidently, my alarm clock had been beeping away for what may have been several minutes. I slapped it off.

"Who am I going to be today?" I spoke the question out loud. After all, there were many versions of Drue. I thought it might be wise to figure out which one I would be before the journey began.

Having been brought to the point of emotional ruin over the years due to the depth and power of my feelings, I had discovered a truth about myself: while I offer "myself" freely to people -- because I long for their acceptance -- I also hide parts of who I am behind masks. If someone -- anyone -- ever wanted to get to know the real me, they'd need a "map to Drue" and several months to navigate it.

The truth is that I had come to feel as though I had nothing much to offer my friends -- or at least, nothing of real value. It's not that I didn't, in reality, have something to offer -- I knew that. It was just that deep down I felt insecure, so these awful thoughts found their way into my consciousness too often for comfort. Any personal doubts I had could easily take hold and grow stronger. On the flip side, whenever anyone said that they enjoyed my company, I often felt a strong pull toward connection.

Connectedness is something I still ache for. Although I have friends and several acquaintances, I've spent a lot of time pondering my worth to others and fighting off the thought that I may never find a deep and enduring intimate connection with anyone. It is a struggle just underneath the surface of my façade, and today it was lurking, waiting for the right moment to turn my excitement for this move into a cluster-fuck of unrealistic expectations and what I imagined would be my inevitable failures.

Music however, is my savior. I powered up my iPod and put the ear buds in. I savored the soundscapes, as lush as any field or meadow, which sprung into existence with a simple touch of the play button. There is a soundtrack to my life, and songs provide a seamless visionary emotional manifestation of it, through my ears. The melodies and bass lines, like the hands of a clay master working magic upon a masterpiece, are incomparably meaningful to me. Music is the puppeteer, and my emotions dance a play according to its will. This day I felt those strings being tugged, as I got ready to begin a new life. "Is that really me?" I questioned myself as I looked into the mirror, freshly showered and attempting to find the gumption to shave.

Blond hair, thinning on top, dark ocean-blue eyes that show the years I've lived, while the rest, all non-threatening 5'8" of me, was as fit and youthful as the gymnast I used to be. I stared at my reflection, identical to the morning before, but with a lingering sadness that made my chin quiver. I recognized my own body and face, but I was not sure that this reflection in the mirror was me.

With a half-imagined "click," I switched my brain to autopilot, knowing that there was much to accomplish before my farewell lunch. There was still a great deal of packing left to do and many calls to make before I could set my wheels...north.

"Funny...," the idea lingered for a moment, "...if you want to leave Anchorage via road you have to drive north for quite some number of miles before you actually head south."

This thought coaxed a half grin from me. I finished my morning routine -- the last one I'd perform in this three-bedroom apartment -- and with one last glance back at my empty room I closed the door, still holding onto my effort-laden smile.

Two hours later, the clicking of my turn signal -- to my ears, sounding like the pounding of a bass drum being hit so hard its bindings were rattling loose -- seemed to mark time as I watched one of my best friends, Kya, wave goodbye and sign to me, "I love you." Richly beautiful, with olive skin, brown hair, and eyes that seem to peer into the soul, Kya is somewhat shorter than me, and a woman with curves who always presents herself with confidence in her body. Confidence -- a characteristic that makes anyone that much more attractive. Just a few strands of her dark brown hair fell over her face, giving her a mournful yet hopeful aura. Her attitude brought me a sense of peace and helped me hold on to the choice I'd made to move. Always supportive of my career in general, Kya was one of the biggest supporters of my decision to take this job that I would have to drive across the country to start. Though it had saddened her, a great deal, to lose her close proximity to me, she loved me enough to really push for this decision, and always told me that it was the right choice.

Her sweetness weakened my defenses against becoming emotional. It is not that I am against being emotional. But I didn't want to change my mind or my direction in life. I was leaving Alaska, and I was not going to change or re-evaluate that decision. I knew that if I began tearing up, Kya would almost certainly cry, and I truly wanted this image of her, peaceful and smiling as she waved goodbye, to be the mental picture that I carried with me for the next several days.

As I turned away from Kya, the reality that I would be alone in my car for close to ten days really started to sink in. I am such a social person. I thrive on human interaction. Fear began trickling its way into my consciousness, taking advantage of my weakened state, and filling my brain with doubt. *What would all this alone time do to me? Could I handle being alone for that long?* These thoughts marched through my mind like a parade of trumpeters.

First a right turn, yet another right, finally a left, and I was on my way. A curious and yet all-too-familiar feeling flushed through me, pushing me close to tears. These streets held such good memories.

Walking home from the bar on Dale St., dancing in the cold, and kissing a girl I had only just met in the middle of the intersection.

I had kissed her at this exact intersection. The memory filled me with elation and warmth. Suddenly, all the memories from all the streets I'd traveled in the four years I had called Anchorage my home flooded in relentlessly, without regard for chronology or accuracy.   Emotions bounced in and out of my mind as if they were on bungee cords, stretched to their max, and then released upon me with unforgiving intensity.

Fighting back tears, I attempted to refocus my attention.

Driving to Talkeetna, hiking Crow Pass, white water trips, bars, dancing, music, videos...

I could barely maintain a thought for longer than two seconds. As I attempted to muster a smile and hold onto just one thought, my tears began. The first chased its way down my cheek, rested briefly on my chin, and then fell to my lap.

I tend to feel things with undeniable intensity. Although this serves me well at times, making me empathetic, it also can cause pain and rob me of my decision-making skills. On more than one occasion I have been sitting and practically staring at the right choice, usually to stop myself from doing or saying something, only to jump at the closest opportunity to fuck up everything.

When I was 23, I remember holding on to a dark and ominous memory that I knew would carry me further down the spiral of depression, but instead of letting it go for other thoughts that were readily available -- you know, any other thought in the universe -- I chose to remain emotionally attached to the least healthy ones, and subsequently ended up in a hospital suffering numerous self-inflicted wounds.

Surprisingly enough, though, this uncomfortable ache, this call to depression fighting for a stronghold inside me, did not sway me in my decision to pick up my life and move 5,000 miles away. Admittedly, my chest felt like an elephant had decided to rest upon it, my shoulders ached, and the sheer number of flashing thoughts, ranging from, "Should I stay?" to "What if I break down on the drive?", carried with them so many strong emotions that I could hardly keep my focus on the road. But, in spite of the questions and despite my shifted understanding of myself, the reality was that I was on my way.

~By the River and Through the Woods~

Many miles ticked away on the Glen Highway as I sat comfortably in my little blue beauty. Brand new, my Nissan Juke was revved and ready to blast out the next ten days and thousands of miles -- just she and I alone. The memory of when we first met played upon my thoughts like a million piano strings being struck at once. Not uncomfortable by any means, but unexpected:

There she was in the brightly lit showroom of the Nissan dealership. I had been shopping for several weeks to find just the right car to replace my aging love, Saphira, a 2007 Pontiac G6.

I always give my cars a name. I think it's because I spend so much time in them, I like to think of them as more than a motor and so many parts. Each one I have ever owned had its own unique beauty, and reflected some part of my personality that I was connecting with.

A bright blue 2011 Juke was poised perfectly under the showroom lights, and sent off sparks of shining color from the high gloss metallic paint, emphasizing her aggressive stance. Sleek, beautiful, and forceful, scorching her lines into my retina, she was the one for me.

Kya had been with me, and she too felt certain that this blue beauty was destined to be my companion. Cora had a stereo system that could keep me planted in my seat, navigation to keep me on the right path, and a turbocharged engine to keep my heart fluttering. She and I were a match made in Alaskan heaven. Her name came to my mind quickly, as soon as I had recognized that she was the right choice. That December day in the snow-filled streets of midtown Anchorage, I met the girl that would carry me to Florida.

Now she was packed from hatchback to seat back, with odds and ends tucked neatly into the passenger seat. She didn't even whimper.

Gazing out of the window to the mountains, with the rain clouds billowing in, I continued to try to keep my mind busy. I focused on anything other than the feeling that I had just left behind all that I loved. I had variable success and moments of failure, and the aching in my gut waxed and waned like waves crashing against the shoreline of a rocky beach. Like a board tide, emotions flooded me with no concern for my attempts at holding them back. Colliding against my will, my feelings overcame me with ease. Just as the mountains must give way to the effects of water, I too had to yield to their infinite power.

Pulling over next to the river, I leapt quickly from Cora as if she held danger. Lighting a cigarette and taking a long deep breath, I released a sigh that carried with it the beginning of yet another round of tears. Thoughts of turning back bullied me, trying to dominate my mind and make me rethink my decision.

The problem was that I was far past being able to turn back. So I stared off at the mountains on the opposite side of the river and pulled a few more drags from my cigarette, feeling the warmth of the half-hidden sunset upon my face. I closed my eyes and waited for the churning in my gut to subside. The fast-moving waters rushing alongside me, opaque from glacier silt, played a symphony in my ears.

For as long as I can remember, I have always loved the sound of water. Standing there with the sun warming my face, the crashing sound of white water filling my ears, and the smoke escaping my lungs, I began to feel the scales tipping in the direction of happy thoughts. This was an adventure, or at least a new start. I'd lived in Florida before -- indeed, I'd been born and raised there. Even though Alaska sings to my heart melodies of majesty and freedom, I knew Orlando was where the money was -- money that would allow me to visit Alaska when I needed to. I'd be closer to my family. And Orlando has more roller coasters than Anchorage. That last thought made me grin.

With a renewed sense of being right in my decision, I flicked the cherry from my cig, threw the butt into an empty Coke bottle, and returned to Cora's comfortable embrace.

Following the weaving road, as though she were as entranced by it as I was, Cora steadily ticked away the miles between Palmer and Glen Allen. My little blue beauty shared with me all the sights and sounds racing by as we pushed closer to our first real stop. Cora gave me freedom and the ability to spontaneously experience adventure. I once jumped into my car and drove until I ran out of gas, just to see where I ended up. Even though she was nothing more than metal and plastic, Cora inspired me.

She was a participant in my journey, and every time I saw something beautiful and awe-inspiring, we stopped. The natural beauty I saw pulled hard on my heart because I knew I was leaving it behind. But we kept going. I switched my focus from knowing I was leaving, and regretting it, to appreciating the beauty I was experiencing.

At that point, it was as if someone had flipped a switch to put me on autopilot. I started staring blankly out the windshield, oddly unemotional. This is a rare state of mind for me, as I tend to be ruled by my emotions. The robotic zone I'd entered somehow helped me to focus more intently on the beauty around me and the road ahead.

Then something weird happened. Watching the wall of evenly spaced trees on either side of the highway speed by and become greenish-brown blurs, I started to notice my peripheral vision closing in on me. The world I saw through my windshield pulled in tighter and closer, until I could only see black asphalt and the yellow lines stretched out in front of me. Panting, I felt my gut quiver, and then I felt the quiver move up my body and shake my shoulders and arms. My heart pounded in my ears. Somewhere in the back of my robotic, autopilot mind, I figured that if my peripheral vision closed in any tighter, I would have to pull over, but somehow, I wasn't worried about that. Then the music I'd been listening to faded and muted, as my hands, wrapped tightly around the wheel, started to tingle and become numb.

"Am I about to faint?" I said out loud, and as I wondered that, one of the strangest feelings I have ever experienced beat into me like the wings of a hummingbird. This new sensation drove its way hard into my chest. I felt a wave of heat, my hair standing on end, and sweat beginning to bead on my forehead. Then something came to me. I wasn't hearing voices, but I felt this thought enter me, and take control. And that thought was this: *Something great is about to happen, and you need only make yourself open and available to receive it.*

Then, just as rapidly as the sensation had come over me, it passed. My senses seemed to reset themselves and became sharp and clear, just in time to see the bright green sign: "Glen Allen 2 miles." My first real turnoff.

Bringing Cora to a stop in the oversized gas station parking lot brought to mind the old adage about men: we don't ask for directions. A slight chuckle worked its way out of my chest. Although I had my AAA TripTik travel planner with me, I was staring at two separate highways proclaiming to be "The Alaska Highway." There was no real way to know which one was actually the right choice, so I sat motionless in my car with a map in my left hand, my phone in my right, and a persistent desire to figure this out on my own. Breaking my glassy stare at the dashboard, which despite its intensity was bringing me no real benefit, I glanced over at the wooden bench perched in a grassy area to my left.

"Clearly, that is a smoking area," I thought, conjuring a desire to exit the vehicle and light up a Marlboro. I did, and the nicotine seemed to wash away the fog and mental smudges that clouded my thoughts, as though it were a bottle of window cleaner. I felt as though I had a beaming light bulb bouncing happily above my head, which had to be evident to everyone hurriedly moving about the parking lot, illuminating the right choice as though it were a neon sign with a large red arrow directing me to "Go This Way." But possibly it was the fact that I could now see a sign that read "Highway 2," just like the highway marked in my TripTik.

~Hitchhiker~

*G*as tank full, caffeine starting to take effect, and back on the road, I felt the lingering sense that there was an impending shift in my life -- that something great was about to happen. Every time I exhaled, the exhale carried with it a cleansing sensation. Swelling warmth radiated from my core. The road that lay before me was rough, and getting rougher, but I maintained the same speed because I felt I was driving myself to a destination of epiphany. Cora navigated the road with ease, as if she too eagerly wished to arrive at a place where something amazing would happen.

Finally, Cora and I reached the Alaska Highway. Coming upon it more quickly than I would have preferred, I hit the brakes and put on my turn signal. The clicking noise reverberated. I could hear it over the loud music blasting from my speakers. The clicking matched the beat of the music, and my heart beat synced with both. I heard it as though no other sound pulsed in the car. It was like Cora's voice, and it reined in the pulsing of my heart, slowing its rapid pace so that I could focus on whatever was about to happen to me.

As I finished that right-hand turn, I noticed a man standing on the side of the road. He had a backpack, bag, and guitar, and a hand held out for a ride. He was young and scruffy-looking. Before I was even fully aware of what I was doing, Cora and I stopped alongside him. Looking at him, I wondered how I'd fit his stuff in my car.

I stepped out of the car and looked down the road to this young man gathering his belongings and heading towards me. At first glance, he looked different than what I expected a hitchhiker to look. But then again, I'd never stopped for a hitchhiker in my life, so what the hell did I know?

He was scruffy, yes, but there was also something different about him. He was wearing a long sleeved blue-gray button-down shirt with the sleeves rolled up, and a pair of dirty jeans. Obviously fit and healthy, he carried himself with a confidence only someone with a fair amount of life experience could have. He was on the thinner side, but tall and he had a very non-threatening posture. I looked at his handsome face and thought he must be used to people admiring him. But there was something more about the way he carried himself. He had something going on -- something that went beyond good looks. I couldn't put my finger on it, or even explain it. I just felt it. In an instant, just like that.

After a quick greeting, I busied myself with some creative re-arranging of the contents of the car, and even more creative finagling of his things. He sat down in the passenger seat and closed the door; his guitar stretched across his lap, and introduced himself.

"My name is Chuck," he said, as he reached out to shake my hand over the Styrofoam cooler.

The tone of his voice was low but not overly deep, and he spoke clearly and confidently, almost formally, like a much older man. It didn't match his youth or his tattered clothing and dirt-stained hands. Somehow, this made me relax. I breathed a sigh of relief as I started to feel a bit more comfortable, and introduced myself.

"My name is Drue, it's nice to meet you," I said. My voice cracked, maybe from the quivery feeling in my chest, or the frog that had suddenly leapt up into my throat. I was so damn self-conscious. But I couldn't help it. I'm just not that brave sometimes.

Chuck had no leg room and was barricaded into the seat with his guitar nestled up against the dashboard and pressed into his chest. Between us the small white Styrofoam cooler acted as an armrest, although not an altogether comfortable one. I awkwardly began to converse.

"So, where are you headed?"

"Tok," he said, matter-of-factly.

Tok it is, I thought to myself as I set the cruise control, turned my attention to the road and tried to think of the right words to speak. I wanted to calm my queasy stomach and the feeling of lightheadedness I had from taking this risk, to justify my decision to stop and pick up a total stranger.

It somehow felt easier to focus on his rugged features than on my own fears. Mentally, I put us into a mortal combat situation. He was taller and stockier than I, but I have speed and an almost uncanny ability to squeeze out of holds when wrestling. He had youth and strength, but I had constant awareness of my surroundings, and I am not so old that I can't defend myself. But it was his eyes that suddenly demanded my attention. They told me he could teach me something, if I was willing to learn.

I stopped sizing him up for combat and glanced at his face in profile. His rounded cheekbones and angled chin didn't detract from his youthful handsomeness. He was unshaven, and while his facial hair was clearly defined and thicker in some spots, it still lacked a sense of intentional shaping. It was an accidental, yet thoroughly convincing, non-beard. His hair was thick and black, and it looked like he'd just woken up and hadn't bothered to comb it. It was obvious he hadn't seen a shower in at least a day or two, but he didn't smell too bad.

Having gone backpacking for several days at a time myself, and essentially living from a sack, I could relate to his lack of grooming and general disarray. It triggered in me a spark of respect as well. His smile and personal warmth made it easy to forget that at that point, I had only known him for 20 minutes or so. It felt like we were old souls re-encountering one another. I felt a wave of happiness well up in me as we connected. It was not unlike the first moment when you see your closest friend after being separated for too many years.

"Where are you headed?" he asked finally.

"I am headed to Florida," is what fell out of my mouth.

"From one extreme to the other, huh?" Chuck laughed.

"Yeah, I guess I like to do things to the extreme," I responded, laughing. "So why are you hitchhiking to Seattle?" Somewhere amidst the small talk we had been having, I had discovered that he was making a pit stop in Seattle, and I was more interested in learning about him than I was in talking about myself.

"I am meeting a good friend of mine in Seattle and we are going to hitch across Canada to New York," he explained, and I could hear a hint of excitement in voice, even though his tone of voice and calm posture didn't fluctuate in the least.

"Wow! Why New York, is that where you're from?" I asked.

"Actually I'm from Boulder, Colorado, but I go to school in New York."

"Really? That's cool, what school?"

"Columbia University."

"Columbia University. Nice, what are you studying?" I asked, but in my mind, I felt as though I might be bothering him with too many questions.

"Physics," he said, and began to explain, but in that instant my mind fluttered off, taking in the fact that I had a brilliant man in the car with me, who was hitchhiking across the country to return to a prestigious school. *Physics major at Columbia. Christ.*

It seemed to me, regardless of my fear of strangers, that I was fascinated by this free spirit who had landed in my path, if only for a brief time, and I wanted him to share his thoughts, ideas, experiences, and distinct perspectives with me. I was unsure exactly how he felt, but I was glad I had stopped to pick him up.

Avoiding the subjects of politics, sex, and religion -- as is customary in encounters with strangers -- we continued to keep things very light. Chuck recounted stories of past rides, while I told him I'd never stopped for a hitchhiker before.

"So I'm your first?" Chuck teased lightly.

"Yeah, I can't even begin to explain why I stopped, but I just more or less felt like I needed to." I tried to explain, but couldn't think of words that would do justice to the feelings in my mind and heart at the time.

For a while we chatted politely, skimming the surface and not going deeper. Both of us held off on crossing any conversational boundaries.

I talked about my work as a sign language interpreter. He talked about the job he'd had in Fairbanks all summer. There was an occasional moment of silence in our ramblings, but it never felt uncomfortable or awkward. Both of us seemed to be enamored with the beauty that surrounded us on all sides, and though the road was rough, the ride was smooth and enjoyable because we were like kids in the proverbial candy store, staring at the sights. The two of us gazed in as many directions as possible in order to absorb all the details we could while traveling at 65 MPH. The mountains were our guideposts, the trees our roadway, and the river our companion, offering us both just what our souls desired: connection with nature.

"The one place I'm looking forward to most is Liard Hot Springs," I said.

"Oh yeah? Why?"

"It's like an oasis. A warm swimming hole tucked away from the world. People stop there to melt away the stress of driving. It's not for people who don't like to rough it, though."

"How come?"

"Well, for one thing, there's no electricity. It's not a place where you find all the modern conveniences you might expect at a tourist spot. But people love it because it's natural, it's beautiful, and the water makes you feel good." I paused. I didn't know much about Liard, just what I'd read in tourist brochures. "I've never been there. So I'm planning on stopping there," I added. Chuck grinned at that.

"Hey -- can I stick with you until we get to Liard?" Chuck asked, glancing at me. "That sounds like too much fun to pass up."

I wanted to say, "Hell, yes." Instead I managed a cool, "sure." Inside, though, I felt a sense of joy and calmness that surprised me. I'd just met him, but I felt a sense of comfort with him that I wanted to get to the heart of. Why was he impacting me this way?

I wanted so much to just let go of all ordinary conversational conventions and blanket him with a million questions, but instead chose to ask just a few, and focus on his answers. I listened to each word he spoke and processed it with as open a heart and mind as I could manage. Oddly enough, this task seemed easier than it had ever been in the past, when I'd made efforts to keep my mind and heart open simultaneously. I took a moment to look away from the road and made eye contact with Chuck. It was just enough to remind me everything was ok. My eyes back on the road, I decided to give him the opportunity to choose the soundtrack for our ride together.

"Feel free to change the music to whatever you like," I said, pointing out the auxiliary port to hook up iPods.

"What kind of music do you like?" he asked.

"I pretty much like everything except rap. But my collection ranges from Irish folk music to Marilyn Manson."

"Whatever you have playing is fine with me," he said as he shifted in his seat.

I lowered the volume a touch so we could talk.

"Why hitching?" I asked, eager to learn more about his willingness to ride with strangers. As dangerous as it felt to pick up a hitchhiker, I thought it must feel at least equally risky to hitchhike.

"Why not?" he countered. "I believe people are good, for the most part, and I like meeting people and learning about them."

Was it surprise, enjoyment that I had met someone similar to myself (or at least the "me" I thought I was that day), or was I feeling a connection to Chuck?

"So what's your favorite thing about hitchhiking?" I asked, my curiosity driving my questioning.

"I've always liked the freedom of it. Out on the road and headed in whatever direction you choose. It's liberating."

My heart lit up with joy at the thought. One day I might be brave enough to do the same thing Chuck was doing.

"It can be a bit much at times," he continued. "You might not get a ride for days and get stuck in the rain. You never really know who is going to stop to offer a lift, but sometimes that's the best part. Really...it's more about the freedom...if you focus on all the other stuff; it just wouldn't be worth it."

"Sounds awesome! I really like the adventure of it all. I mean, I just started backpacking a couple years ago now, and…," I said, struggling to find the words I wanted to use. There was still so much of myself I needed to keep hidden. Why? I am not sure. "…I don't know," I continued. "I love getting out and enjoying nature and having everything I need right there on my back -- out in places that few people, if anyone, have ever seen. I think…"

"You are pretty freaking brave," Chuck interjected.

"So what's the worst aspect of hitchhiking, then?" I asked.

Chuck flashed a quick smile, "Well, you never really know who is going to stop to offer you a lift."

I smiled. Though, admittedly the smile may have been more evidence of my nervousness abating than it was of understanding his perspective on the matter.

"Like, this one time," Chuck said, his posture changing as he began to recount the story, "this guy picks me up, and as I open the door to get in, several beer cans come falling out. Once I took my seat and shut the door, I realized they were freshly emptied beer cans and the man was trashed."

I am certain my disbelief was apparent. "Wow!" I said.

"Yeah, I asked him if he wanted me to drive, and oddly enough, he was all for it," Chuck replied.

I'm not altogether sure what Chuck said next because I was wondering what I would have done in that situation.

It's difficult to describe the manner in which I assault myself internally at times. I have one hell of an active imagination, and I am unfortunately prone to use it against myself. My daydreams, nightmares, and vivid recollections -- though rarely even bordering on reality -- do have one thing in common: I am always "not good enough." Not good enough to save myself, or not adequate enough to succeed, or I am just simply left, calling to mind the phrase, "You have been weighed, you have been measured, and you have been found wanting." Elaborate scenarios of negative outcomes can manifest in mere milliseconds in the firing synapses of my brain. Stories of loss, violence, and movie-like dramas enter my mind as though they were actually taking place. I can discern what is real and what isn't, but there are times -- most times -- when these thoughts trick my body into responding as though it were all really happening. I am in a constant state of "fight or flight," one might say.

So as Chuck spoke, I was imagining a thousand different outcomes related to hitching a ride with an intoxicated man from Alaska. Most of which were not pretty.

Surprisingly enough, even though I was severely distracted, I was able to pick up on a few of the points Chuck was making. Despite my surreal visions of drunken car accidents and late-night arrests, I gained a basic understanding of Chuck's life in Fairbanks. He had an internship in the weather and science center at the University of Fairbanks, and it sounded like more fun than work -- or at least by his smiles one would assume so.

Time had gotten away from us, as can happen in conversations sometimes; neither of us noticed that the sun had made a dash for the west and was setting. Summer was aging by this time, and sunsets had begun to occur once again, leaving a faint memory of the day painted in the sky.

After a quick pit stop to dispose of the cooler and re-pack things for better riding comfort, I began to feel more comfortable with the idea of having this rider in the car with me for at least a couple days. The minute that I decided that, I began to feel more relaxed. We made the appropriate telephone check-ins, knowing we would soon have no cell phone signal. Then Chuck and I fit ourselves back into the car and headed northeast to Canada.

~Horror Stories, Potato Chips, and Beer~

Just past the United States border, but before customs check, Chuck asked, "So what story are we telling border security about us?"

Story?

"Huh?" I spluttered, suddenly feeling an uneasy lump in my throat. I felt, once again, a little out of my comfort zone picking up a hitchhiker. It hadn't occurred to me that crossing the border might be a problem.

"Border patrol doesn't really like it when you say you've picked up a hitchhiker," said Chuck, although he didn't seem worried. He explained that not having a prepared story might make us look suspicious.

"What if we say we met over the summer and are sharing a ride back to New York?" he said, throwing out the idea.

In complete agreement -- not that I could have disagreed anyway, since I had absolutely no clue about these things -- we set out for Canadian customs with our stories straight, his passport in hand, and my fingers crossed. Somehow amid all this, I think the two of us, in cahoots, with a lie to tell the border patrol, started to feel like buddies.

As we drove past the "Welcome to the Yukon" sign, he pointed out that it is written in both English and French. Because almost anything starts a conversation when you are getting to know someone, this comment instigated a discussion about languages, both the ones we knew and the ones we wanted to learn. In the midst of this exchange I discovered Chuck was learning German, already knew Spanish, and he, like many others, thought ASL was a universal language for Deaf people around the world. Actually, most people I meet believe that American Sign Language is used in other countries too, and they are usually quite stunned to learn each country has its own signed language. Chuck was interested to hear about that.

The "Approaching Customs Reduce Speed" sign stood out visually, like someone wearing a pink shirt in a sea of navy-blue, grabbing my attention. Following each sign's instructions to the letter as we rolled through customs, I looked over to Chuck, again very briefly, and he handed over his passport. With the window down, seat belt secured, radio off, and everything in its appropriate place, I was prepared and had a smile on my face as we approached the border patrol.

"Hello, bonjour," the man said in a quieter-than-expected, friendly tone of voice. He spoke clearly enough for us to understand without straining.

"Your passports, please," he continued, and although I knew this was not really a request *per se*, he made it sound as though it was with the polite tone of his voice.

My stomach turned in all directions except the right one and I swore I could feel his eyes burning into my forehead, eagerly anticipating catching me in a lie.

"Where are you headed?" he asked.

My mind quickly flipped through the story Chuck and I had agreed upon.

"New York," I answered simply.

Without even raising an eyebrow to glance at us further, the soft-spoken man continued. "How long will you be in Canada?"

"The plan is no more than four to five days." My voice faltered just slightly when I realized he was staring hard at my passport. Quickly, my over-active thoughts began a rapid onslaught, and I wondered why he was hesitating while looking at my passport and not Chuck's.

"Are you carrying any tobacco or firearms?" he asked. His third question set my mind at ease. Clearly the previous answer, despite my hiccup in pitch, must have been the response he was looking for.

"I have nearly a pack and half of Marlboros, and no sir, I do not own a gun."

After I made this declaration he handed our passports back, and with a gentle smile wished us well on our way.

As we slowly pulled out from the small building, Chuck and I looked at each other in amazement at the total ease of the encounter. I know I certainly had anticipated it to be a bit more detailed, or something far more complicated than it actually was. I have to assume Chuck felt something similar because his facial expressions were not all that different than the ones on mine.

"Simple enough!" I exclaimed. We moved on.

"Damn, I was hoping he would stamp my passport. I don't have a single stamp in it yet," I said while leafing through my empty pages, smiling.

Chuck's passport was filled with stamps from all the various places he'd visited, and I felt a bit of envy wash over me for a moment. I was older than he, but I hadn't had any international traveling experience.

"I was expecting so much more," I continued, with mock exasperation.

"Well, you can always turn this car around, go back, and ask him to stamp your passport!" Chuck laughed.

Both of us continued to laugh and make light of the situation as we distanced ourselves from the border, but I kept my eyes on the rearview mirror, just to be sure the polite Canadian border guy didn't change his mind about us, and fly up from behind. Once safely down the road a stretch, I transitioned from worrying about the border crossing to the fact that it was getting close to 10:30 p.m. and we had not established where we would be setting up camp for the evening.

Eventually we stopped at a small town inn.

"God, I smoke too much," I thought to myself while lighting yet another cigarette.

Chuck had ventured into the lounge, which was conveniently attached to the inn. We'd decided to stop for the night and we were both ready for a beer; or six. The two of us wanted to camp rather than pay for some overpriced hole-in-the-wall hotel room, so Chuck questioned the woman inside about the best place to locate a good campsite, and this freed me up to stand out by the road and enjoy the fact that I smoke…a lot.

What was it in a cigarette that seemed to ease the uneasiness -- to blanket my nerves with warmth? Like reminiscing with a long-missed friend, each drag brought me in deeper to the connection it held within me.

My attention shifted rather abruptly to a passing car, and I couldn't help but take note that it had been the only car to pass by in at least 15 minutes. I don't know why or even how the thought filtered its way into my brain, but I was struck by the disturbing feeling that I would be sharing a campsite with a man I hardly knew, and there wasn't a single person who knew where I was or even that I had picked up a hitchhiker. Despite how our fledgling friendship had grown over the hours of driving, I had a rippling sensation of fear, which flowed back and forth over my entire body. Like those circles that radiate outward when you throw a pebble is into a body of water, the fear came in waves. Maybe I had allowed the fact that I was enamored with Chuck, and loved learning about someone new, to cloud my judgment. Suddenly the choices I had made before that point started scaring me a little, or at least enough to stir my overactive imagination. I started breathing shallowly. Just as panic began to creep into my consciousness, Chuck stepped clear of the shadows cast through the parking lot with a six pack of beer, a smile, and directions to the lakeside camp.

There was a calming feeling he exuded, and I felt defenseless against his smile and my desire to know more about him. All my uneasy private thoughts faded. Once we were back in the car, I focused on the road and the directions he was telling me. There was a black road, black sky, and darkness spread throughout. The drive was eerily discomforting, but I kept a smile on my face and my breathing as close to normal as possible. Just about 500 feet from the established road and camp grounds, Chuck pointed out there would be a turnoff that would lead us down a dirt road, but he thought that my car could "probably" handle it.

Of course she can, she is Cora! I thought to myself, trying to ease my own fears.

Tucked interestingly off the road and behind overgrowth, the road had no name. We would have mistaken it for an extended shoulder if we hadn't received directions that indicated this was the turnoff to camp. The shadowy road and hidden view did nothing to assuage my fears. Catching a few potholes on the drive down, I watched the brush run tighter and tighter to the rough path -- really nothing more than a glorified ATV trail.

Dipping closer to the lake and circling back up to hillside trees and small clearings, we continued to drive further from the main road as the lights from the car disappeared quickly in the thickening shrubbery. My heart started beating harder, and I could have sworn that Chuck heard it, but only acted as though he couldn't out of respect for me. I started remembering scenes from horror movies in which unsuspecting travelers follow the directions of seemingly innocent and nice young ladies, who in reality are setting them up to be in the right place at the wrong time so they can be abducted and tortured by backwoods crazies who get their kicks by disposing of stupid tourists. I could see large knives, twisted men with missing teeth and overalls -- scenes straight out of a B-grade horror flick you pay two dollars to see on some random Sunday night.

"Damn, I need one of those beers," I giggled under my breath, hearing the bottles clinking together each time the car hit a pothole.

Cresting a hill and making a bit of a left downturn, we came to a clearing, a rather awesome clearing, complete with a large open vista to the lake that, though we couldn't see it at the time, would make a great scene in the morning -- or a great place to be murdered, if that was how the cards got dealt. I found myself thinking that maybe I could swim away to safety if required. That thought lasted only a second, when I countered it with the fact that no one survives in water this far north. Not for more than a few minutes anyway.

We decided that this was the right place to camp. Chuck and I began unloading tents and other camping gear, preparing for the night. We both noticed serious signs of rain, and predicted it would be coming sooner rather than later.

"You ever see *The Hills Have Eyes*?" I asked as we unloaded our gear.

"Yeah," Chuck half laughed as he looked over to me, "why?"

"As we were driving down here, I couldn't help but think about different scenarios that could play out here, like scenes in that movie. You know, with someone giving us bogus directions, and setting us up to be murdered." I tried to keep myself from sounding too serious as I spoke.

I couldn't believe I'd actually shared with him the overactive worry that I would be the unsuspecting tourist caught up in a scheme perpetrated by the locals to rid the world of dumb travelers one stupid American at a time. With a bit of a chuckle, then an odd abrupt stop in mid-movement, Chuck looked me straight in the eyes and politely asked, "Does it bother you that I have a knife and bear spray?"

Before I could catch the words that blurted from my lips like an over-eager child ready to take his first plunge into the pool, I stated, in a solid, matter-of-fact tone, "No, I trust you."

Not even a tenth of a second passed and my brain started wrestling with the statement I had just made. *Did I really trust him? How could I possibly trust someone I had only just met? What the hell is he thinking about me since I said that?* Considering that I thrive on the acceptance of others, his opinion almost mattered more to me than anything else. The tornado of crazy thoughts and "what if's" took hold and attempted to run me further down the slippery slope of my cascading emotions. The way that my emotions can sneak in and slap me around so quickly that I barely recognize what's happening, truly puzzles me.

Stop! I exclaimed emphatically in my head. *Just fucking stop. This is a time to enjoy life, not obsess over the stupid shit.*

With a dumbfounded surprise at the fact that this little self-talk actually worked, I changed gears mentally and continued setting up camp.

Tents up, beers open, and fire started, we sat close and discussed the coming drive and other random stories.

"What inspires you to write songs?" I asked, looking across the fire to Chuck sitting Indian style as he drank his beer.

"Pain mostly. Different situations, really. Life. Girls. Breakups," he answered with little hesitation.

"I believe I can relate," I responded after a slight pause. "I tend to write a lot of poetry and most of it is centered on difficulties or painful times in my life."

"I know what you mean," he said. He took a second, as if to catch his breath. "I am trying to find other inspirations for writing, but it seems difficult."

"I know. I always seem to go back to darker places in my writing," I continued. "It's like I am watching myself going through these things but am not actually a part of it, like I am an observer."

A bit of a longer pause in the conversation cropped up and gave both of us time to be mesmerized by the fire as we shared a bag of chips and sat quietly. It was amusing to me that Chuck was able to start a fire with damp twigs and brush gathered from around our site and subsequently this caused a hint of a smile on my face. Not to mention the potato chips had to be some of the best damn chips I'd eaten in years. I guess that's what happens when you're hungry. The small yet healthy fire burned with an ever-so-familiar and welcoming scent that lured my senses and brought back memories of past camping trips and backpacking journeys. I love the smells and sights a fire produces. It is intoxicating; with an ability to bring me to a trance-like state that I could enter for hours simply by sitting next to a camp fire.

"I wrote a song I think you might relate to. It's called *Clown*." Chuck broke the silence just as the first drops of rain broke free of the passing clouds.

As I peered at him across the small pit made from lake rocks and sand, Chuck appeared almost menacing, or maybe it was my imagination at work, playing tricks with the lighting and small sparks that billowed up from the weakening fire. Yet I was so intently focused on his story about why he became a musician and how he gets his inspiration for songs that I was only dimly aware of the panic that was starting to grow within my gut, churning away like carnival food does when you eat too quickly and take one of the spin-you-around rides at a state fair. Chuck had an openness that I found ensnaring, and I could hardly take my eyes from his silhouette while he spoke, even though at times the orange-red light cast on him seemed haunting. But when he began making a connection between the ways I had spoken about my past and the themes in

Clown, something in me clicked. This somehow set my fears to rest and brought me back to the moment.

"I could sing you a line from it," he said, but it almost sounded like a question.

"I would like that," I replied instinctively.

"And we're grasping at some forgotten past, that makes us act like fools, but we're lucky 'cause there's many of us and we've all got shoulders too. So when your pants are down, remember how, we all get cycled through," Chuck sang.

He had such a strong voice, with just a bit of a rasp to it, yet it was also a voice that you could easily listen to and then drift off into your own thoughts, while staying connected with his presence. Music, especially emotionally charged compositions with relevant and heart-tugging lyrics, can bring a pleasant ache to my core which feels like a mixture of infatuation and complete serenity. I was not sure whether it was the timbre in his voice, the kindness of his demeanor, or the vulnerability he showed, but I was overcome with an emotion that settled all the uneasiness I had previously felt. I could feel his lyrics physically, as though my hair were standing on end, but internally. The feeling rushed to my core and filled my heart. I could relate. We could relate. Maybe this was going to be a good drive, if

I continued to have this kind of soul journey for a few more days.

"Maybe...," the thought echoed in my head like the sound of a church bell traveling the expanse of an entire city, and then bouncing back, "...maybe I will learn more about myself through the process of learning about him."

Sharing that bag of chips for dinner, and drinking our beer, Chuck and I sat across the fire from one another, but I felt a feeling of closeness that warmed me equal to the flames that flickered in front of me. Peering up into the sky for a moment, longing to see stars, I caught a raindrop from the darkening clouds that shifted in shape and position -- almost more quickly than the eye could perceive. Heavier rain was soon to be a cold reality, so we got into our tents.

The sound of raindrops is amplified exponentially when the it beats upon a tent, and my ears were also playing out my childhood fears of hearing a creature in the distance growl in time with the rustling of trees, which didn't help matters.

"So let's get this straight," I actually verbalized these words loudly enough for me to hear, but not enough to be heard outside my tent. "Chuck has a knife and bear spray...you have a can of pressurized air that makes a loud noise...a fucking loud noise...really?"

In a frantic motion that was almost comical in its absurdity, I sat up in my tent, which pulled my sleeping bag up with me, and because my pillow was tucked into the top of the bag, it brushed against my back unexpectedly.

You know that feeling when you are absolutely sure you have just felt death touch your shoulder and there is not a single thing you can do to escape its clutches? That feeling in your heart of sheer terror intermingled with the thought, "Holy fuck, I'm not ready to die yet"?

That does not do justice to the panic that stupid pillow caused as it fell away from my back to the floor of the tent. I can't tell you why I didn't let out a panic-driven barrage of curse words, but as the rain continued beating upon my tent and my heart slowed back to a normal pace, I started to listen to the soft sound of Chuck shifting in his tent, and his snoring gave me something much less intense to focus upon. He clearly felt at ease around me.

Eventually, I actually passed out, but having exhausted myself with horror stories and a racing mind. The dreams that followed played out all of my previous fears but in a wildly more erratic and graphic manner. In one dream, I found myself standing half naked in the pouring rain, bleeding from a large wound in my abdomen after wrestling with a buck-tooth, buzz cut sporting hillbilly and speaking out to the heavens, "I wonder what color the water is." I fell to my knees realizing my car-mate had been murdered. "I bet it's a beautiful shade of blue."

Panic made me rocket up from the sleeping pad, grasping my chest, and I coughed, nearly choking on my own saliva. I could see trails of light following my every movement, as though I were on a mild acid trip.

As my vision returned to normal, I heard the faint sound of Chuck, just a few feet away, snoring as he comfortably slept, and I felt myself relax again. "It was just a nightmare," I told myself.

Since I was not able to fall directly back to sleep, my mind wandered to topics of love, relationships, dreams, and goals I wished to attain. *Who am I really? Why do I feel the need to hide myself? How is it that I've arrived at this place in my life?* Question upon question bounced in my consciousness like a ball thrown into a room full of fine crystal. Although my thoughts didn't feel quite as urgent as they had in the past, these queries left me with a feeling of emptiness growing within my chest. My heart was still beating a bit faster from the sudden interruption of my slumber, but I was surprisingly less affected by it than I'd thought I would be. Normally, my nightmares destroy any chance of returning to a relaxed state, and rarely allowed me to drift back to sleep. But it seemed tonight would be different.

Cradling my head into my right arm, I stretched my left out to retrieve my cigarettes, I lit it quickly and just listened to the softening shower that weakly continued outside my warm tent. Chuck's lyrics repeated in my thoughts and before long I had forgotten about the nightmare and its graphic nature. Hours passed slowly, but I was thankful for the privilege of experiencing the passage of time at all. The time to experience new things; the time to be alive; the time to accept myself, whoever I may actually be.

And with those thoughts I flicked my Marlboro from the warm, dry confines of my tent and welcomed a return to slumber.

~Day 2~

"The vast and the open, and what's seen in dream.
Of the sun and the moon, and what lies between.
It is a distant place that beckons me home.
The place in my heart where I am never alone."

~A Quest for Breakfast~

Morning brought with it a feeling of freshness and cleanliness that stirred my heart as I gazed out onto the lake. It was much like I had pictured it the night before, when I had stood in the same spot trying to make out the features which were now so plainly visible. The trees and overgrowth parted perfectly before me like the waters of the Red Sea where Moses struck his staff, creating a frame through which to view the wonders of nature displayed in quiet serenity.

"The water *is* blue," I half-chuckled as I thought to myself, staring out over the lake. "More a gray-blue because of the darkening sky, but blue nonetheless."

I can't really identify a specific reason for my desire to look at this particular lake and confirm its shade. But I am glad that I was able to gaze upon its beauty before the rain started again and distorted its glassy sheen and crystalline color.

Chuck was still asleep and although clouds remained, the rain took a reprieve. I took the opportunity to relieve myself, emptying my bladder as I gazed off into the distance and pondered the day ahead. Getting breakfast was the first priority, overshadowing most other thoughts, with the exception of my observation that darker clouds were just starting to float in off the horizon. Allowing Chuck to continue his peaceful rest, I gathered my belongings from the soaking tent that had so sturdily protected me through the night and began packing them up again.

I began mentally reciting the lyrics of multiple songs, as it appeared my stomach could temporarily be satiated by their emotion-stirring effects. For some reason, I found myself repeating lines from *Clown*, and although I didn't remember them perfectly, I connected with the feelings they aroused and I was energized.

Now ready to dismantle my tent and finish packing things back into the car, I leaned down in front of Chuck's tent and attempted to speak his name as a sort of pleasant wake-up call to the brand new day. Remaining there for a few moments, unsure of exactly how to wake him, I stumbled over words and phrases like some school boy who had been called to stand up and recite the Gettysburg Address. Nothing louder than a muted "uh" escaped my lips for several minutes, when finally I managed a simple, "Chuck," and then lingered a moment for his response. He replied with a groggy "uh huh," and because I was still at such a loss for words, I re-tasked myself to packing the car and gave him time to awake.

When he got up we began working as a team, breaking down camp together. Since we were equally eager for breakfast, the undertaking was rather hurried. It probably helped that the rain was beginning to return as well. Safely back into the car, all belongings nestled in and our camp site appropriately cleaned up, we hit the dirt road back up to the highway and headed off in hopes that the next town wouldn't be too far away.

More miles passed than I had hoped we would have to endure, considering that we both longed to fill our stomachs with good old-fashioned breakfast food, and a quick glance down the dash revealed that Cora was also hungry. Things wouldn't bode well for us if we didn't get her fed soon. Mild concern grew into worry as I watched the gas gauge lights dip ever closer to that dreaded E, which somehow seemed much larger than it ever had in the past. Chuck was checking the map again, no doubt because he had seen the worry that had appeared on my face, and he assured me we were not far from the next small town.

Almost like magic, a blue roadside sign came into view: "Kluane 2 km." I was certain my sigh of relief was audible, but truthfully at that point I was so happy that both Cora and I would be fed that I didn't care how I sounded.

The Yukon is pretty freaking awesome, I found myself thinking. My sudden burst of enthusiasm may have been due in part to being grateful that a gas station in a small town like this was full service. I was completely charmed by the older man at the station we pulled up to, as he stepped from a much older building, limped his way to my car parked up next to the pumps, gave me a warm welcoming smile, and began to fill my little blue beauty without my ever having to touch or say a thing. *Wow!* I thought.

I was also struck by the beauty of the stunningly majestic mountains and ice-blue waters of the abundant lakes all around us, and I was anticipating breakfast like a ravenous lion released from captivity into a den full of docile sheep.

Still further it could have been some variation of all these things rolled up into a genetically altered mutant-like thought process which had become self-aware and was now planning total world domination…after breakfast of course.

No matter the reason, I was pleased that the older man was very kind and not only filled the tank but offered us advice on the best place to stop for food. The only unfortunate thing was he announced that breakfast had stopped nearly an hour prior. *Damn time change!* I had forgotten about setting my clock an hour ahead to account for the new time zone. Still, any food in a restaurant sounded good, and the opportunity to be out of the car and off the highway for a spell didn't sound half bad either. Thankfully, Chuck agreed to stopping.

The restaurant/inn was situated on a dirt road next to one of the many cool blue lakes that surrounded us in this beautiful landscape. Clearly an older building, the restaurant was rectangular, and true to classic rustic form, it was painted dark brown and had wood carvings and swinging screen doors that really brought a personality to it. Perched as though on guard for the property, an interesting handmade bear, evidently carved from darker driftwood, sat just to the right of the main entrance and peered down on all who entered.

As we walked in through the door, it was obvious to us where we should sit: right next to the windows that looked out on the lake. The water was a shade of blue that only lakes tucked away in rugged mountains have, a color that is unique yet somehow seemed familiar to me as I stared out across the lake to the farthest shoreline against the towering mountains. I was hypnotized by the small waves, barely larger than ripples, which were a beautiful mix of blue-gray and turquoise, and failed to notice that our server was standing patiently waiting for me to order my beverage.

Chuck was having coffee and I -- not that anyone would or could expect anything different from me -- ordered a Coke. Caught between looking at Chuck as he recounted stories of past hitchhiking experiences and gazing off into the lake's mesmerizing blue, I felt I had arrived at a place free from the passage of time or responsibility. Not that I really had any major obligations pressing for my attention, other than arriving in Florida by the 29th. It was just nice to feel completely unaffected by time.

For me, time had usually felt like a monkey sitting on my back weighing me down in the race of having or doing all the things that others had or were doing. Prior to my move to Alaska, there were few moments in my life when I was content with simply "being." Moments when I was not preoccupied by what was or could be happening, or focused on daunting tasks that required my attention, instead of feeling this simple, unabashed reverence for the moment I was living and with no actual regard for how much time I was spending in it.

The non-breakfast we had ordered progressed well with equally shared conversation and laughs, coupled with map-checking to see just how far Liard Hot Springs really was. Peering down at the map situated on his place mat, Chuck appeared to be in deep thought, and then raised his head slightly to ask, "If you don't mind, I will stay on with you 'till we reach Dawson."

Of course, there wasn't even the slightest bit of a chance that I would say anything other than yes. I looked up from my own map and replied confidently, "Sounds great."

Even though I was relaxed and enjoying the peace of a morning without the usual time crunches and work obligations, a slightly off-putting thought speared its way into my consciousness: *Chuck will only be riding with you 'till Thursday.*

Not that I expected him to be with me the entire ride down to Florida, but somehow Thursday just seemed really damned soon. Too damned soon. Thankfully, this thought retreated to the back of my mind just as quickly as it jumped in, and I was able to re-engage myself in the moment.

We ate the last bites of food slowly as we both continued looking out to the waters that washed up only feet from the deck directly outside our window. Once we both had achieved the satisfaction of a full stomach and serene state of mind, it was time to exit this friendly

Canadian diner and return to the highway that called out to us, "Ride hard to the springs."

Chuck figured we could make it to the springs that day, albeit kind of late, so he convinced me it would be better to keep going until we got there, since we would then have more time to enjoy it the following morning. The kind expression that softened Chuck's face made me drop any protest I had against driving late into the night.

After a quick check of the car to see how well it was loaded, I turned to Chuck while lighting my cigarette and noticed that the carved bear was staring at me with an expression that said, "You must take a picture." Subsequently a tourist moment took place and we were both laughing as we clicked off a few shots. Saving a picture of Chuck specifically to send to Kya as soon as we had cell services again, I explained how well he fit her definition of scruffy attractiveness. He volunteered to up the ante by roughing up his hair and making sure his shirt was sufficiently unkempt for an additional shot. Several more moments of laughter followed.

This is the best kind of morning, I began thinking to myself, as we stepped back into the car and I hit the push-button start. Just a few turns and a drive of about one kilometer later, we arrived at the faded asphalt highway which would run under our wheels for the next several hours. A brief glance back down the road to the gas station, a half-smile and a nod to Chuck, and we were off. The sun then made a brief appearance from behind one of the many clouds billowing through the area, and I was struck with a sudden burst of emotion that I could barely contain.

"I am really glad I stopped to pick you up!" flew out of my mouth with barely a thought forming the words.

Chuck looked over to me with a grin that really showed his youth and vibrancy, and said, "I am really glad you stopped to pick me up too."

~Opening Up~

We had a wide open road, wide open spaces and only the sporadic car passing us every 20 minutes or so. I set the cruise control to 100 km per hour and set my heart on arriving in Liard before the end of the night. Chuck was examining and critiquing a friend's writing, while occasionally looking up German conjugations. I was peering steadily out the windshield at the passing hillside landscape that blended up strikingly to the mountains that all had various-shaped cloud halos cresting them. Like strictly enforced boundaries, the rain came in patches that oddly went from dry to full-on downpour without a warning.

This time of quietness gave me the opportunity to reflect, ponder, and being my typical self, to over-think. Given this tendency, I was struck by a thought that had previously been in the back of my mind, but which now pulled its way to the forefront as though it were scaling the cliffs of my subconscious. It was bent on keeping itself from being forgotten or becoming less powerful. That thought was that everything I was currently enjoying would only be around until Thursday morning.

To stop that thought from taking control, I quickly conjured up a question to ask Chuck. I had hoped to start a conversation that would redirect my excitably active brain. Metaphorically my fingers were crossed and with a bit of luck, maybe I could push that thought off a cliff and allow it to plummet to its demise.

"What's your best and worst hitchhiking experience?" I asked aloud, and then thought, *Wow! Did I really just ask that question -- again?* It was a chastising thought. I had asked the question as though I'd forgotten what his answer was the first time. Worse, of all the questions to ask someone, this one suddenly seemed utterly childlike, when I'd been longing for deeper, more mature discourse. "And he already answered this question, you dumbass," I mumbled under my breath as I attempted to chase away the reddening of my face with a quick sip of my Coke.

Setting aside his papers and evidently quite willing to answer, Chuck settled himself in more comfortably and began his story.

"The best would be when a girlfriend and I were traveling together across the state and this group of guys picked us up. This being her first time, she was pretty scared," he said, and I could see his countenance shift as he spoke.

"We were packed in tightly in the back seat with another guy and there were three rough-looking men sitting up front too. We were tired from a long day of walking on the highway and we didn't get much sleep the night before, so Stephanie laid her head on my shoulder and we both just stared out the window, listening to the classic rock the gruff men were blasting out. There was almost a romantic feel to it all; it was one of those moments you never forget."

He recounted the story as though it had just happened, and I couldn't help but think that Chuck and I were very alike in the way we held on to memories. The ability to remember images and sounds accurately, to feel as though you are experiencing the moment again, is a skill that might not be unique, but it felt like a bond connecting me with Chuck's immensely positive energy.

"The worst? Well, other than spending hours or even days out in the cold rain and not getting a ride? Actually that's harder." The quizzical look upon his face brought a silent chuckle to my throat.

"One of the more interesting, but somewhat odd experiences, happened recently. Remember I was telling you about the guy who picked me up drunk and I ended up driving?" he asked.

"So he did let you drive, then?" I quickly replied, to let him know I had been listening.

"Yeah, all the way into Valdez," he responded.

Chuck went on to tell me the details of a number of his experiences: more about driving the drunken man to Valdez; about being picked up by a group of guys toting rifles and several handguns; and meeting a woman who chain-smoked pot. The stories made me think about who I wanted to be: a free spirit, able to adapt myself to any situation and live as though time held no sway in my life. I found that the more time we spent together, and the more that Chuck elaborated on his life story, the more fascinated I became by him. Mind you, I had not lived a boring life by any stretch of the imagination, but there was something about the way he described his meanderings and travels that made me feel completely spellbound and almost envious. I longed for his youth and unfettered outlook, for if I were to be gifted that indulgence once again, I'd be doing exactly what he was doing.

I am not sure how much time passed, but my bladder made it clear it was time to stop, regardless of whether there was a place to pull over. Hitting the flashers and coasting off onto the shoulder, I brought the car to a halt and cast a quick glance over to Chuck that announced,

"Cigarette break." With unspoken agreement, we both got out and lit up. There were no trees or brush just off the road, but this did not stop Chuck from unzipping his jeans and relieving himself.

"The world is our toilet," he jokingly exclaimed.

My first instinct was to quickly turn away, but instead I tilted my head in a "oh-well" manner and chuckled to myself, "He's right."

With this, I pivoted away from him, turned my attention to the rugged tree line in the distance, and unzipped as well.

Becoming lost in the beauty before me was no more difficult than taking a breath. The clouds, floating above the multilayered line of trees, created mysterious shapes and scenes not seen by any other soul. Out here, we two were the only audience and the universe played beautifully for us. It wasn't until I heard Chuck approaching from the other side of the car that I realized I had finished peeing but was still standing like a statue.

Pacing near the car, stretching, and for good measure checking to make sure that my bike was still tightly secured to the back of the vehicle, I couldn't help but be amazed at the splendor that surrounded us. Looking past us and out to the horizon, I could see a patchy gravel road with two solid yellow lines that faded off into the clouds as though the road was a highway to the heavens. No sounds, no cars, nothing blocked our view of the road as it shrunk into the distance, seamlessly connected to the blue sky and gray clouds that hovered above us. As far as the eye could see, it was only us and this road, and I was so completely contented with this fact, I almost shed a tear.

I was thinking to myself that I really wanted a picture of me standing in the middle of this pathway to the gods, to capture this perfectly picturesque moment, when Chuck approached and asked me to take a picture of him in the same spot. Obviously, my reply was yes, and I asked for the same in return.

Interestingly enough, the first car that passed us in more than an hour came when I was trying to snap a picture of Chuck in the road. Even more surreal, it was an ambulance. I was briefly distracted, but Chuck's smile and the ever-shifting kaleidoscope of sky and clouds quickly pulled me back.

Pictures taken and cigarettes finished, we were overtaken once again by the desire to set more miles behind us. We were solidly back on the road for more than 20 minutes when the rain began another assault on all that was around us. With the low atmospheric ceiling and sheets of raindrops pouring onto the windshield, we could no longer see the beauty that had been overwhelming to our eyes. Instead we saw barely recognizable shapes hidden amongst floating oceans of dark grey clouds.

But then, as if to offer recompense, the universe then gave us a sight magnificent to behold and exceedingly rare. I got Chuck's attention by slapping his shoulder with the back of my hand, and drew his line of sight to the double rainbow that descended from the heavens and came to rest nearly dead center of the road ahead of us. The first rainbow was one of the fullest I had ever seen, with colors radiating brightly and with a strength that caused it to appear almost solid. The second, slightly smaller and just a bit weaker in its intensity, made a vibrant display across the sky.

"It's a double rainbow!" Chuck exclaimed in a mocking voice, and proceeded to act like he was crying.

"It's just so beautiful!" I replied with equal mockery in my voice, followed by an almost identical fake cry.

Both of us laughed and quickly brought out our phones to start snapping pictures of the wonder before us. Rain bounced off my windshield in large heavy drops, while the sun tried with all its radiance to break clear of the whispering billows of gray. In the distance the brightest of the rainbows landed in the road and it looked like our path would carry us directly to the pot of gold. Unfortunately, there was no gold guarded by a spritely leprechaun, but driving through the mist, bathed in the bright colors of refracted light, felt like reward enough.

The weeping clouds continued to send their showers in a cyclical pattern so precise that we could almost guess when the next one would start or cease. Half of the time it was raining only hard enough for the moisture to dampen the world around us. But at other times it was more like God himself had opened the skies, changing His mind about flooding the Earth a second time. During this time, without knowing why or how, Chuck and I started talking about religion and politics, and our once rather careful conversations began taking on a depth I found intriguing.

"More spiritual than religious, if I had to categorize it," said Chuck, responding to my question about his religious beliefs.

"I don't see anything wrong with people that want to believe in something so much that they worship an invisible entity that requires faith that he even exists," he continued.

"What are your religious beliefs?" he asked me calmly, after a few moments of silence.

Looking out into the great wide open spaces left from the glaciers, I held my breath for a moment, knowing that what I felt and what I told myself to believe were two different things, and wondered how I could explain myself without sounding like a complete dimwit. An oversized U-shaped bend to the road in front of us drew my attention off briefly. We were in the valley of a long extinct glacier and approaching its final resting place. The mountains rose to either side of us and narrowed in on the road like giant gods of the universe standing in judgment of the damage we had caused. Jagged cliffs crashed together in a boulder laden snow-chute. This was where the ice no longer carved the rocks. The mountains had won and the glacier was gone. Its remnants, still visible from the finger-like streams, trickled out from the rough terrain. They webbed their way down and out into the valley which opened up widely to our left.

"Well, I was raised southern Baptist, but I couldn't be further from that now," I began.

"I go to community churches, because I really don't believe in beating someone over the head with a Bible and condemning them to Hell just because they don't believe the same things I do." Oddly enough, the words seemed to spill out of me with progressive ease the more I spoke.

"I cannot stand people who run around thinking they are holier than everyone else because their religion is right and all the other people out there are wrong. I don't believe in preaching hate and will not tolerate a pastor that uses the pulpit as a place to propagate that kind of bullshit." *Wow*, I thought, *when did I become so fervent about this topic?*

"I know I have much to learn and I try, more now than I did in the past, to keep an open mind about things. Because I was raised by my father in a Baptist household, I do have strong beliefs about some things, but I am also willing to set those views aside, knowing that I may tend to lean in that direction 'cause it is all I know, and that I could actually be wrong..."

"I know exactly what you mean," said Chuck, half interrupting me, but during a pause in my sentence that lent itself to someone making an interjection.

"I feel the same way about life and learning," he said. "We are raised by parents with specific beliefs and ideas of right and wrong, but as we grow and learn for ourselves we find that sometimes what they believed is not necessarily what we believe."

His words cut through me and hit the core of who I am and what I wanted to say, although I lacked the mastery of the English language in that moment to express it.

"You are right," I quickly replied. "My father may not have been the best father in the world, but he did what he could with what knowledge he had and I don't think at any time he did things out of malice or a desire to see me fail." A knot began swelling in my throat.

"He is a strong man. Physically speaking, but also in his opinions and the way he expresses them. He is also a bit short-tempered, so he comes across as very angry and mean at times, but I think now, looking back with different eyes, he was teaching what he knew the only way he knew how." Again, I paused. There was so much more I could share about the depth of hurt the relationship with my father had inflicted upon me, but this was not the time for those words.

"That is good that you can say that now," said Chuck, filling the silence left by my pause. "I think you're right. Most of us are molded in ways that will always be a foundation for our beliefs from our parents, or whoever raised us, but we need to venture out into the world with a mind that is willing to absorb other truths and compare them against what we know and believe and adjust accordingly. It is only when we refuse to budge that we become slaves to thought processes that are archaic or blind."

Our conversation continued from there to delve into topics like our current President, oil, gas prices, and our penal system. Neither of us stopped exploring the other's point of view, but there were times we disagreed. I don't remember the words we said or many of the details of the dialogue, but I felt that there was a convergence of the beauty surrounding us and the intimacy of the discussion we were having. Interestingly, as I listened to Chuck, I found that his beliefs could not have been further from those that I was raised with, yet I agreed with him more than I disagreed.

Listening to his words also gave me the urge to research the points he was making. Whether through continued conversation, reading, Internet research, or other means, I wanted to access enough information to know I had a firm grasp of things and all the layers involved, to make a decision to change my views or remain the same. And at that moment, I was leaning towards making a change.

If there was one thing I discovered on this journey, it was that my beliefs had been molded quite solidly by my father. This is not to say that they were right or wrong, but that they were his beliefs, and for far too long I had just accepted and echoed whatever he believed without regard to what my heart -- or the facts -- said to the contrary. Especially when it came to religion and politics, my father's beliefs had a strong influence on what I professed to be my own beliefs. I felt that a paradigm shift was in order, and that this was the time to move in that direction.

Experiencing this modern marvel, the Alaska Canada Highway, with an open heart, dilated mind, and a new friend, I found I was looking forward to the long road ahead and all that these internal reflections were revealing. We had another strong dumping of rain, so I slowed my speed and focused a bit more intently on the patchy road rushing underneath us. The sun was setting, and cast a brilliant glow onto the clouds in front of us.

It was one of those moments that you want to take a mental picture of, and hold onto it so that you will never forget it. I knew I would not allow it to escape my memory any time soon. Not only because of the beauty sprawled out before me, or because I was experiencing this whole new perspective on my beliefs, but because I felt utterly free. Released from my emotional bondage, able to feel and to express those feelings openly, and free to explore who I really was in safe company. All of this caused my heart to swell with elation and a sense of grateful bewilderment at the opportunity I'd been given. In an odd moment of providence, Chuck looked over at me and said in a heartfelt tone of voice, "This is really cool."

"Now I know for a fact that this is something I will remember forever," I said, and felt a slight flush and reddening of my face. Though my words were strictly spoken to myself I almost thought, simply due to their strength, Chuck had heard them.

I believe he must have felt that our friendship was growing more intimate, too, because his part of our discussion continued to deepen and become more personal. Progressing, evolving, shifting; the words we spoke and topics we addressed constantly took on new shapes, just like the sky had earlier in our drive.

"Do you believe a man can be raped?" Chuck asked. The question surprised me, but given the fact we were discussing my insecurities about women and having my virginity stolen at a young age, it was far from random.

"I do believe a man can be raped, yes," I answered, knowing I had more to say on the topic.

"There is a difference between stimulation and arousal. Just because a man can get an erection, it doesn't always mean he is interested in having sex." I stumbled on these words, even though I knew the point I was trying to make. "If someone convinces someone to have sex or manipulates their way into having sex when that person is not giving full consent, then it is rape. It doesn't matter if it's a girl or a guy or any combination thereof."

That sounded so much better than I thought it would, I thought, as I paused for a moment to see where Chuck wanted the conversation to go.

"I believe I was raped," he half mumbled but stated clearly enough that there was no mistaking his declaration.

I remained silent for another minute, partly because of the fact that if I had tried to speak, I believe I would have sounded like a moron, and partly because the knot in my throat would not allow any words to pass.

"There was this girl...it was a weird night," Chuck continued. "Met her at a bar and ended up at a house party after a blues jam, checking out the local dives and a marijuana grow-op in a cabin. Everyone was drinking and we were interested in each other. Either way, the next morning I remember thinking that I really didn't want to have sex with her and she was pretty adamant about doing it regardless of my thoughts or opinions on the matter."

This was the most disjointed sentence I had heard Chuck speak in the entire span of our time together. I don't know what I said next. I know that I continued to speak, but it was from a wordless place. Feelings. That was all. The words were welling up from a place that doesn't need words.

Minutes dissolved into hours and kilometers sped by, as we both continued to open up about our past, our goals, and every so often explore more light-hearted fare, such as stories about drinking or past indiscretions. It's not that I wasn't paying attention to the specific words he was using -- certainly I was -- but my focus was on the feelings the conversation aroused in me. I couldn't help but marvel in the feeling that I was not alone.

In the middle of a sentence, Chuck suddenly stopped and announced that he wanted me to hear some of his favorite music. I felt an even deeper connection to him. To me, sharing music is like sharing a part of one's soul.

I'm not talking about the everyday shit you might throw on or plug into, but the music that makes you think, or cry, or touches a part in your soul that only you know. Sharing that kind of music is like opening a window to an immensely privileged territory inside a person, and that has an equally immense, profound effect on me. He played several songs from a genre called "post rock" that was intriguing to say the least. It reminded me of Sigur Ros and Bon Iver. The songs were longer than the typical rock or pop song, and they tended to be built with layers that you wouldn't find in most of the trash heard on the radio today. I say all of this to mean: I liked it, very much.

Chuck explained the songs as we listened, and was clearly very eager to pick the next artist to share. That he showed a fevered interest in his choice made me feel more connected to him, and from the first note, the next song that he played was my favorite. Chuck fiddled with his iPod which was connected to my stereo, turned up the volume and the interior of Cora was filled with the soundscape of "Jackie Says" by Mono.

I say "soundscape" because that is exactly what powerful music can do: create a moving image in my mind, like a video presentation of the feelings and emotions being evoked by sounds. I can respond like this to music across all genres, whether the song has lyrics or not. "Jackie Says" is completely instrumental, and it grabbed my heart from the very beginning and refused to let go. It was a simple song but complex in the emotions it stirred, and I felt my heart beating in my chest, the hair on the back of my neck stand on end, my arms tingle, and my hands begin to tighten upon the steering wheel. I had completely succumbed to the power of the music pumping through the speakers in my car.

There are no words or expressions that could adequately describe that moment. Deeper feelings than a song had ever been able to pull from me aroused longings in my soul, as though small electric charges had been sent in to awaken the sleeping and re-animate the numb. Somehow, as I looked out into the ever-darkening evening, I realized I was relating to this song so deeply that I felt I would be permanently moved by it.

Once again, the rain began to crash against my windshield, and my heart continued beating like a school boy's leaning in for his first kiss. Then the guitar and piano started their decrescendo, and all at once I felt that all was right with the world.

Really? I thought to myself. *Do I really believe that corny-ass statement? It's just a passing moment.* I continued to try to rationalize my way out of my feelings. But now, thinking back, I would argue that for those few minutes at least, while the newness of my perceptions still lingered, all *was* right in the world.

~Dinner and a Moose~

*E*ven when there is nothing else to see; dusk in the Yukon is an absolute beauty to behold. The shifting of colors to a muted blue; the haze that blurs sharper edges down to soft curves and long lines, it was a wonder that I was able to drive at all. The non-breakfast we had consumed nearly 500 miles ago, and the light snacks meant only to tide us over, had long been digested. Only nicotine and caffeine remained in our bodies.

Thankfully, from what we could see on the map, we were only a few kilometers away from the next town. It was our chance to refuel ourselves and the diligent Cora. Watson Lake was the name of the town, and it sparked my memory, although I could not put my finger on why. This was actually the fourth time I had traveled the ALCAN Highway, but it was the first time I had done it alone, with much greater awareness of the road. When I was seven my father drove us up this long stretch of desolate gravel to Anchorage. We left just two years later, and the journey back down filled me with sorrow. The third time was an interesting several days following behind my dad's Buick Century Limited. Now, on this historical stretch of World War II ingenuity, greatly improved over the years, I felt a strong relationship to it. This was no ordinary road, no simple two-lane highway to carry commuters. No, this was a lover, a fair lady with curves and beauty that could not be matched. She had opened herself to me and gave me sights and feelings only a few would know.

Watson Lake! Now I remembered it. This was the town with the park in the middle that was made up of license plates. It was called Sign Post Forest, if I was remembering the name correctly. We were officially nearing the end of the Yukon Territory and entering British Columbia. I felt a pang of sadness briefly touch my heart.

"We should buy some stuff to eat for tonight. I wouldn't be opposed to buying some beer, too," I said. Chuck agreed.

I pulled off at the nearest gas station/grocery store on edge of the highway, and we made our way inside as the rain came down a little heavier. After several trips up and down each of the aisles, we decided on salami sandwiches, chips, and cucumbers. Oh, and little to no discussion was needed when we realized they sold liquor. Captain Morgan and 7-Up was on my menu and the menu was good.

When we were just outside of town, edging ever closer to the BC line, we stopped to fix our food and rest before pushing forward onto Liard. Chuck was rather handy with his knife and made damn good salami and cucumber sandwiches faster than my stomach could release another growl. Dill and sea salt chips rounded off our dinner as we watched the remaining light fade away into the pitch black that quickly engulfed the roadside pullout. As Chuck speedily sliced up the ingredients for another couple handheld tickets to heaven, I rattled off several anecdotes from my work interpreting, and read aloud short stories that I'd saved on my computer.

I realized then that I wanted to make damn sure I shared as much of myself as possible. I wanted someone else to see and know Drue. Not the Drue I would have chosen to be if this morning had been like all the others. Not the me who carried several different masks in his back pocket just in case the one he wore became thin or transparent. No -- this was the Drue who loved every moment he was spending with the hitchhiker from the Glen Allen turnoff. The me who enjoyed hiking, backpacking, techno music, and dancing with Kya. The man, which for the first time in as long as he could remember, felt he had nothing to hide.

Darkness had now fully covered the land and we got back on the road. I drove at a steady if not slightly dangerous pace. Maybe it was my cockiness about being a good driver, or maybe it was that I wanted so badly to reach our destination, but I drove with my eyes set on the road but my mind envisioning things far removed from the present place and time. We spoke sporadically, and exposed the vulnerable spaces carved out in our memories. But for the most part we were silent as I listened to the music and stared out at the darkness that stretched beyond the reach of my headlights.

When Chuck spoke again, he spoke quietly, but with buoyancy, which continued to move and elicit a response from me. It felt truly odd to be able to speak about things that I'd never told anyone else with a person I had only known for couple of days. Hitchhiker therapy? It seemed crazy, but the more time we spent in the car conversing, the more I felt a comfort with Chuck that helped me to reveal all the wounds I would otherwise have kept covered and hidden. Words seemed to form themselves into sentences, and then fall easily from my dehydrated lips (those sea salt chips had done a number on me!). Not a single force in the universe could have stopped my emotions from welling up and spilling over, starting after our roadside dinner stop and continuing during the stretches afterward of talking and reflective silence.

"I have always felt an immense amount of shame for the things I did to gain access to drugs," I said slowly, as though allowing the statement to filter out at a reduced speed would allow me time to retract the words if I felt or saw Chuck's posture change to a more judgmental stance. We had navigated the conversations to past regrets.

"Selling, pawning, or trading things to get my next fix really ate the humanity from my soul and left me feeling worthless and hateful." Although a tear tried to escape my eyelids, I fought it back.

"I actually sold my body for…" I couldn't finish the sentence and tears began to course down my face.

With a look of concern and genuine care, Chuck leaned in towards me and spoke with pointed but careful words.

"Everyone makes mistakes and look what you have achieved now. You are not that person anymore; you are so much more than a memory of past errors."

I don't believe my therapist ever made this much progress with me in such a short amount of time. I felt the freedom of complete openness, very much like the old clichés of having the world lifted from your shoulders, or a great weight removed from your chest. As much as I despise these tired phrases, they were wholly relevant to what was transpiring.

I switched between my high and my low beams to adjust to the rising steam and dust from the road, and as a result my field of vision was sometimes clear and sometimes muted. Perhaps I should've taken this as a sign that I was driving slightly faster than I should have been. But my thoughts were more on our conversation than the highway ahead of me. I wasn't fully aware of what I was seeing in my peripheral vision when I spotted something large moving just outside the reach of my headlights. Almost as quickly as the instinctive thought came to me that I should slow down, Chuck shouted "MoreAHHoose!"

Well, really it was more some concoction of a completely unrepeatable word, something like, "horse," and "moose," but I knew what he meant, because that was when a young bull moose galloped right out in front of us.

It was too late to do anything but lay on the horn and hit the brakes, and I pushed my foot to the pedal as though I were trying to shove it completely through the floor and use my feet on the asphalt below, like something from a "Flintstones" cartoon. I veered off to the right and just barely missed hitting the moose, which had zigzagged its way onto, then off, the road in front of us.

Pure luck spared us from having an accident, but in that adrenalized moment my twisted imagination filled my mind with terror. It was as though a Super 8 film clicked away on an old projector, rattling with images grainy and distorted, yet somehow clear and vivid enough so that their colors and content would be burned into my brain for many nights to come.

In my mind I saw the moose crashing onto the hood and rolling up into the windshield, its weight easily destroying all in its path. I saw blue shards of steel turning into ginsu knives, slicing and dicing even more smoothly than they do on the infomercials. My body ached with every imagined horror, like some psychological experiment gone horribly wrong. The whole of the moment passed like an oversaturated re-enactment played in fast forward.

It all ended with Cora grinding to a stop on the gravel road. She now looked more like a Salvador Dali painting than the fresh aggressive design she once was. I found myself in a state of shock, looking up to the clearing sky and catching sight of the Big Dipper, and thinking abstractly, *It really is a beautiful constellation.*

My heart rate had gone from, "Hey, chill, man, we're smoking hookah on a Sunday night with a bottle of black label rum," to "Holy fucking shit, man, can I have another 12 dozen red bulls and vodka?" in a matter of milliseconds. My brain still registered an eternity of madness but I also knew that it was only in my mind.

This duality of sensations made me physically shake, a fact that was readily apparent to Chuck. In that moment he reached out and touched my arm. I felt it was a gesture initiated in hope that physical contact might be calming. Laughing, with a tone of surprise and relief, Chuck was muttering something my ears could not register due to the overwhelming amount of blood pulsing through my body. My head throbbed, and the sensation was like someone placing a steel pot over my head and beating it repeatedly with a spoon.

Thank the gods there is a pullout, I thought. *A nice, safe, moose-free pullout.* I could pause for a moment and allow normal bodily functions to return, and while I was at it, I could have another cigarette.

Not really leaping from the car, but getting out rather quickly nonetheless, I lit up a smoke, took an extended drag, paused for a moment, and then, as if releasing the smoke from my lungs could also carry out with it any lingering shakiness, I exhaled with a force that made my breath audible. It was dark on the road with the exception of the faint glow from Cora's parking lights and the occasional red flicker from the cherry of our overpriced, not even partially comparable to Marlboro, Canadian cigarettes.

"Holy shit, I swear I actually saw us hit that damn moose! It was fucking intense!" I blurted out to Chuck, who was standing opposite me on the other side of the car.

Still half laughing, he asked if I was okay. I answered with a simple, quiet affirmative, and we both continued smoking while gazing up into the dark sky speckled with stars.

Not much time passed before a semi-truck rolled up into the pullout. Chuck immediately opened the car and began rummaging through his backpack, then calmly shut the door and placed the contents of whatever it he had been searching for on the hood. I didn't have any idea what he retrieved and he maintained such composure that I barely pulled my eyes from the stars above us. Once the 18-wheeler had come to a complete stop and the engine ceased to rumble, Chuck looked over at me and held up his bottle of bear spray, laughing at himself.

"I guess all those stories you were telling about crazy people and horror movies have got me a bit paranoid," he said.

"Really?!" I managed a half-laughing response.

"I tend to believe that by nature people are good, but for whatever reason, I guess your elaborations on the theatrical scenarios got me thinking -- or over-thinking," he admitted, as he set the bear spray back in the passenger seat of the car.

It struck me in that moment, as Chuck softly let the passenger door close, that throughout our conversations, he was really listening to me. It wasn't just a polite façade to appease the driver who had picked him up. This made me feel good.

"Did you see that movie, *Joy Ride*?" he asked as the interior car light faded.

"Yep, sure did. I really like horror movies in general," I said as I exhaled another drag from my smoke.

"There was another one very similar to that...uh...I can't remember the name but it had a twisted trucker in it...." He paused again.

"*The Hitcher*?" I asked. Somehow that title seemed very funny to me considering Chuck was the first hitchhiker I had ever picked up.

"No, not that one, but one very much like it. Of course, I guess all of them are pretty similar if you really think about it."

Ducking behind a tractor trailer, Chuck excused himself, the only sign of his whereabouts the red of his cigarette as he pulled another drag from it. *Right idea*, I thought, and walked a few paces in the opposite direction to relieve my bladder as well.

I was no longer shaking, and was beginning to feel the call of the highway ahead, as well as the desire to resume our musical exploration. Looking up into the starlit sky, I left behind all of the thoughts that had been making me so scared. And when I looked over to where Chuck was standing, I could tell he was doing the same thing. Over the past few days I had been experiencing one of the warmest, most inspiring feelings of acceptance I had ever felt, and at that moment the feeling was growing inside me again at an exponential rate. I didn't want anything to interrupt this flood of sensations filling my soul, so I stood frozen in place and continued to watch the night sky as though it were a living work of art.

Pondering the thought for a moment, I concluded that perhaps it was just that.

~Emotional Music~

About an hour after our encounter with the moose, we were still sharing music and past experiences, eager to learn more about each other.

"Are you familiar with the 142 bus?" Chuck asked with excitement in his voice.

"Which bus is that?" I replied.

"Do you not know about the bus in Denali?" He looked at me quizzically as he pulled his attention away from the iPod.

"Oh, you mean the bus from the book *Into the Wild!* -- yes, I am familiar with it and I've wanted to make that hike several times, but never had the opportunity." A bit of enthusiasm entered my voice. "Why do you ask?"

"It is a pretty exciting hike and one I highly recommend. If you get the chance and are back in Alaska, you should make it out there," he said.

I could hear the earnestness in his voice as he spoke and knew that what he was saying was important to him. This was something that he wanted me to experience.

"I remember watching that movie and ended up having to call off of work for two days following. It jacked me up something fierce," I said.

"Why's that?" Chuck's right eyebrow lifted a bit.

"Well, you know, I can't quite put my finger on it, but I believe it's because this guy, fed up with the bullshit in life, wanting to experience something real, jumps out there and does something only a few people in the world could or would do." I remembered how the last scene in the movie choked me up with a typhoon's worth of feelings and regrets.

"I guess it's something that I've always felt I wanted to do. Not hike out to some remote place and die, but rather, really live. Just live on what I had and enjoy all the different people, places, and experiences the world has to offer," I continued.

Chuck shifted a bit in his seat as if to be even more intent on listening to what I was saying.

"But really, what messed me up the most was the last thing he wrote in his book, in the movie of course -- a line that really struck a chord in me that I feel vibrating to this day: 'Happiness is only real when shared.'"

When I said those words, it was like a floodgate that had been closed for many years was opened. A sudden wave of emotions engulfed me and I felt my breathing quiver and my throat tighten up. I didn't think I was going to cry, but I felt the sensations that lead to an all-out rainstorm of tears, and that storm was near the surface.

"I think the whole thing really made me feel like I want to be sure I live life and enjoy it, but make sure that in doing so, I don't miss something vital. Like, on the one hand, I wish I were brave enough to just up and leave all that I know and go out and live in the moment, but on the other hand, I really believe in that last line about sharing it with someone." As I said this, I started feeling greater control of my emotions.

"Like you, out hitchhiking across America essentially, and basically going with the flow and allowing life to lead you where it leads. I want that freedom, that sense of adventure," I continued.

"But didn't you tell me about quite a few hiking/backpacking trips you've taken, and whitewater adventures, as well as climbing peaks and other mountain explorations?" asked Chuck.

"Yeah, but…," I said.

"No, I think you have a lot going for you and a lot that has happened to you. If you really take notice of who you are and what you've accomplished you'll see you are freer than you allow yourself to feel," Chuck responded. "And look, you picked up me, your first hitchhiker, and you never thought you would do something like that, so clearly you are working on yourself and your old ways of thinking and perceiving. I think you should give yourself some well deserved credit." His tone of voice was both concerned and encouraging.

"Tell me more about bus 142, if you don't mind," I said, eager to get myself out of the spotlight.

He did, and I found that with each story Chuck recounted, I gained respect for him and felt a deeper sense of peace. I believed deep in my center that nothing harmful or hateful or even remotely unpleasant could happen. I felt that we were surrounded and somehow safely guarded by the universe, allowing us the freedom to share our insecurities and pain in a place free of condemnation. Although our stories were different, we had so much in common. Once again, I felt that ever-growing sense of connectedness, which came to me like a half-recognized scent that lingered close by. It gave me a stable and consistent feeling of belonging that I felt would not leave me anytime soon.

After we talked about bus 142, music again became the focus of our conversation. We agreed that some music could elicit a strong emotional response and even touch our souls. Chuck reached for his iPod and started playing a song that he admitted freely could bring him to tears. I listened to this song with more focus than I had any song since last we played "Jackie Says." Looking at Chuck's face, I caught a glimpse of his vulnerability. My best efforts at describing the moment would fall miles short of exactly how it was coming to life, but the emotion plainly written on his face was unmistakable in its lucidity. He appeared to be longing to experience something from his past, his chest shook, and although he turned his head away to avoid total defenselessness, I saw tears well up in his eyes and fall from his eyelids.

The song's title was "Home," the same title as one of the few musical compositions that can easily draw a tear from me. Watching Chuck without actually turning my head in his direction, I could see that the music was carrying him back in time to a memory that his soul clung to. I did not think it was a sad memory by any means, but it was certainly one that could pluck his emotional strings, quite powerfully. If I were to hazard a guess, I would say that the memory must have made its way into one of Chuck's own original compositions.

As the music faded, we allowed silence to hold for a moment, and the car was filled with the aura of past times masterfully evoked. As we rested in this aura, I felt that

Chuck must be feeling the same connectedness I had been feeling. I felt that the energy pulsing out from him was in sync with the energy I had inside. I continued to feel this way until he broke the silence.

"I've had control of the radio for the majority of the day," he said. "What do you want to listen to?"
I decided to share with Chuck my own "Home" song, the one that reverberated in my soul the same way that the song we had just listened to did for him. He agreed, and so we listened to it together. As it played, my thoughts returned to Chuck's eventual departure. I knew I would feel great sorrow, but I also knew there was nothing I could do or say that would change that course of events. I accepted the inevitable with a slightly heavy heart, as I knew that I would miss him greatly. But I would not allow that fact to ruin the rest of the time I had with him.

~Transpersonal Experience~

*C*huck and I were so caught up in music and storytelling that we began to believe that we had somehow already passed Liard Hot Springs. Chuck broke out the map to figure out where we might be and how much further the next town was. Almost as though it had been waiting for that exact moment, a little blue sign appeared in the glare of my high beams, informing us that there were only 2 kilometers remaining before we arrived at our destination.

I felt a sudden sense of accomplishment wash over me. We had traveled many, many miles that day -- substantially more than I'd originally planned for -- and I was thankful for the time I had been gifted with such a great passenger.

Fuck yeah! I thought to myself, after uttering a more family-friendly exclamation out loud. Not that I needed to watch my vocabulary around Chuck, but I think part of me didn't want to seem quite so childishly excited about making it to the springs.

It was 12:30 at night, and understandably the gates allowing access to the recreation site were closed. Fortunately, across the street was a rest area/ pullout/

everybody-who-didn't-want-to-pay-to-camp-squats-here area, and it had enough room to accommodate us. And rather nicely too, I might add. We circled the gravel clearing and once I had focused my headlights on a spot that we decided would be the best to set up our tents, I killed the engine and popped the hatch.

As we pulled our things from the car, both Chuck and I confessed our dismay at how wet our equipment had remained after we packed it away following last night's downpour. We worked diligently to create a dry space where we could rest our heads for the night, using light from our headlamps and the car. Just as I was setting up the poles for my tent, Chuck looked up to me and somewhat hesitantly said, "I don't want to sound presumptuous, but would you mind if I just slept in your tent tonight?" I responded with a quick and welcoming yes, while thinking to myself, *You didn't even need to ask.*

I mixed a quick drink with the bottle of 7-Up and the Captain Morgan we'd purchased, sipping it as I finished setting up camp. Then, yep, you guessed it, decided to light another cigarette. Chuck followed suit and so we were soon relaxing on an abandoned wood pile. It appeared to be made up of rather large pieces of a boardwalk, torn up and left to rot. Even though I didn't like these Players cigarettes as much as Marlboro lights, I liked the familiarity of smoking in and of itself. It was like a calm collected conversation with a kindred spirit, traversing places only the universe knew directions to. It was raining again, but I didn't mind that very much, anymore. I was catching a mild buzz so very little could bother me.

It was difficult to make out our surroundings because of the darkness, but I could see that the wood pile we were using as our throne of relaxation butted up against a line of rather tall trees. Their shadows dwarfed everything that surrounded us, so I knew they were pretty awe-inspiring -- and I was sure they would be even more so in the morning when I could actually see them and not just their shadows.

I could also make out the highway, or rather the clear space it made amongst all the vegetation, and surmised that the entrance to the Liard recreation site was just past that. As I paused for a moment staring into the pitch darkness, I felt something arousing in the bottom of my gut. It was like two parts anticipation and one part fear had become a volatile mixture within me.

Brushing it off as nothing more than alcohol taking advantage of sparse food consumption, I turned my attention back to Chuck who was swigging his Captain and

7 from a water bottle, with a distinctly mischievous grin plastered upon his face.

"Wanna go exploring?" he asked.

With a nod toward the open spaces I had recently been gazing at, I smiled my response and we both started walking into the night.

The gate leading in was closed and locked, but since it was such a small gate, it was easily navigated even though we had a buzz, so we continued on in hopes of discovering the hot waters of a pristine spring, where we could relax our tired bodies and enjoy the remaining portions of our rum. We saw many -- and I feel the need to reiterate, *many* -- signs warning us about bears on the trees and walkways along the path we were strolling. They were hard to read -- there were no lights -- and this fact made the warnings all the more unnerving to me. I was not all that keen on being mauled while traveling to my new home in Florida. Imagine how that would go over with my family -- finding out that I had been breaking and entering a recreation site and subsequently shredded to the equivalency of human ground beef by a hungry grizzly, while spending time with a mysterious hitchhiker in the middle of the night a full day ahead of my original schedule. Oh, and with the evidence of alcohol in my system -- or whatever was left of my system to check.

Wait... I argued with myself, *why the hell do I care what my family thinks of me and my schedule and what I am or am not doing?*

Rain, albeit not heavy rain, still danced upon us as my thoughts continued to race, playing out all the different scenarios that could happen. It might not be the norm for a man my age to give two shits what his mother, father, and stepmother think of his drinking/ trespassing/ mischievous behavior, but that's what came out of my frightened mind.

"Fuck it! I am having fun!" I whispered sternly to myself, and took another sip of rum and 7-Up. "I...am...having...fun."

It was especially dark because Chuck and I were not using headlamps -- we didn't want to get caught trespassing. Needless to say, this lack of illumination caused us to take many wrong turns, and we ended up in several areas that only deepened my fears. As we stood on a path some 30 minutes after we began exploring, Chuck looked over to me with an expression I couldn't make out, and in a half-whisper asked, "I think that other trail leads to the springs, you wanna go try and find them, or prefer to go back?"

Hesitating, I stood still for a moment and answered with a question, "What do you want to do?"

Chuck laughed a little, as though to signal that he knew that I knew exactly what his preference was: to go on. With little delay, we set out to find the other trail. My heart raced, my breathing was elevated, and yet somehow I was having a blast.

We made jokes about my apprehension for bears and being mauled while wandering around the woods in the middle of the night. The combination of laughter and liquor kept the mood jovial, until at last we discovered the trail that led to the springs. It was a boardwalk, made of the same planks of wood that we sat on after we put up our tent. *They must be refurbishing the boardwalk*, I thought to myself -- or maybe I said it out loud.

Then, as we walked along in almost complete pitch darkness, I thought I saw something moving just ahead of us. I panicked, but my fears were quickly put to rest when I realized it was just a couple who were returning from the springs themselves. This set my mind at ease, because they were coming from the area we were headed to, and they were not running and screaming while being chased by some large grunting animal hell-bent on consuming humans that just had been nicely basted in sulfur from the springs.

Or so my intoxicated imagination kept seeing it: the springs were the bear's slow cooker crock pot.

As we turned a few more bends and navigated through some taller brush, we finally saw ahead of us the changing rooms next to the hot water springs. The springs were occupied by two men throwing a green glow stick, like a game of catch, and laughing about some story or joke that had evidently just been told. We could detect the telltale scent of sulfur from the springs, lifted by the rising steam from its surface. Setting our belongings in the covered changing area, Chuck and I readied ourselves for entering by lighting a smoke. Together, we breathed in the strong mingled scents of the fresh-fallen rain on wild shrubs, the pungent odor of the sulfur, and the pleasantly stinging aroma of Marlboro lights.

After we shared the last few hits from one of our only remaining American cigarettes, we stepped off the dock to the stairs that led into the shallow waters, and allowed the heat to melt away all of the fears that had previously stained our thoughts. The effects of rum and the heat were blurring my perception of things, but not to the point that I couldn't clearly tell what was real or only a figment of my imagination. But I felt that the line between the two was rapidly diminishing.

As he entered the water, Chuck introduced himself to the two men playing catch, and we quickly learned that they were merely driving through, like Chuck, on their way back to college. Literally the second after they had introduced themselves, I had forgotten their names, but I would not soon forget their laid-back, inebriated demeanor. They were both taller than I am and built like quarterbacks. We discovered that they were from Colorado, the same place Chuck is originally from, so a "who lives where" and "do you remember this place?" conversation was instantly struck up.

I remained quiet for the majority of these exchanges, and found myself entranced by the little green glow stick that the men were tossing, as it floated through the air and landed briefly by of the men, then took flight back across the water and splashed down next to the other. Maybe that rum was having a bit more of an effect than I thought. I was not sure if my childlike fascination with this green water fairy was apparent to those around me, but I broke off my fixed concentration and looked up instead to the half-moon that was struggling to break free of the rain clouds and cast its brilliant glow upon us.

I stopped gazing at the moon when the two men left the water and tossed over their green projectile. We said the appropriate "Nice to meet you, travel safe" sentiments, and then we were left alone in the thermal wonderland with our only light sources the struggling moon and that little green water fairy.

I back paddled away from Chuck a short distance, floating in what felt like a completely weightless state, and let my emotions simply wash over me, like the heated water that caressed my skin and kissed my face. It started again, that feeling, that odd sensation in my gut that resembled anticipation and longing, a mixture of desire and contentment. This feeling is something words just can't explain, but my heart and soul completely understood. The two meshed as if they were long-lost lovers finding each other, alone in the dark, in a remote land thousands of miles from anywhere.

I re-centered myself by placing my feet on the soft pebble floor of the springs and then a spontaneous thought jumped into my half intoxicated mind. Before I was fully aware of my actions I had removed my boxers and set them on the dock stairs. Declaring my state of nakedness to Chuck, who was sitting one flight of stairs further down the wooden deck, I floated back out to the center of the swimming hole and continued to drift weightless. Cradled in the heated pool, I watched the sky for signs that the moon might win its battle with the clouds. Then Chuck said something, but because my ears were covered by the warm water, I could not hear him. I guessed that it was something related to skinny dipping because now he was standing up and removing his athletic shorts.

Something uncomfortable sprung up inside me briefly. It lasted only seconds but it was enough to make me quickly turn my eyes away from Chuck. I knew -- or at least I thought I knew -- that looking at him might seem awkward or incongruous. When I looked back, Chuck had placed his clothing on the stairs behind him and had turned back towards me to step further out into the water. As he melted into the hot sulfurous water, the moon triumphed over the clouds and cast a small bit of light on his thin yet defined naked form. He was truly a striking young man to behold. Without feeling anything specifically sexual behind my glance, I could simply acknowledge he was a well formed male figure whose body was easy to admire.

I continued to circle my hands just underneath the surface, pulling in the warmer water to splash against me, and let my eyes wander to and from anything that caught my interest. I longed for this moment to last indefinitely, but much like life feels to one who is drawing their last breath, it was ephemeral. Chuck was closer to me now than

I would have believed I could be comfortable with, given my state of mind and nudity, and I noticed that he was trying to speak to me but with my ears still submerged I could not make out his words.

I stood up in order to better communicate, and looked him squarely in the eyes, for longer than I had for the entire trip up to that point. Although I somewhat fumbled my words, I managed to say, "Coming here has been so much more than I thought it was going to be, and it is that much better because I have someone here to share it with me. Thank you."

Giving me one of his warm youthful smiles, he held eye contact with me and responded, "I'm glad to be here too."

Realizing that if Chuck hadn't joined me I wouldn't have made such great time, and wouldn't even have arrived at the springs until the following afternoon -- thus depriving me of this extraordinary moment -- I felt blessed and inspired.

We stood together, close enough for me to feel Chuck's energy radiating out from him, and looked up toward the moon. The light that it radiated outlined a dark nimbostratus in the sky and danced on the leaves of the trees that surrounded us. I felt another stab of worry that our close proximity was not appropriate because we were both naked -- emotionally as well as in the physical sense of the word -- but then I reminded myself that Chuck didn't seem to have an issue with it. It couldn't be all that abnormal.

I gave myself permission to be okay with everything that was happening and everything that I was feeling. I kept my gaze on the sky above and remained shoulder to shoulder with this strong young man I had grown to admire so much. I was thrilled not to be panicking simply because we were so close.

I relaxed and my mind drifted. I could see in my mind's eye an infinite number of dreamscapes, inspired by the sensory explosion of sights, sounds, and feelings I was experiencing. I envisioned mountains so immense they could touch the stars above us, meadows of flowing grain that cast purple and gold from the setting sun, warm beaches with water so blue it could be sky, and sky so blue it could be the ocean. All of these visions included Chuck, who was standing so close to me I swore I could sense his soul. I could hear a line from the poet Charles Bukowski repeating itself within the millions of firing synapses detonating in my brain: *Be on the watch. The gods will offer you chances. Know them. Take them.*

Only then did I recognize that stirring in my core, that swelling emotional feeling which was over stimulating all my exterior senses to the point of revelation. The entirety of that moment went mute and I was reminded of the promise the universe had given me: *Something great is about to happen, and you need only make yourself open and available to receive it.*

As the rain fell on my exposed skin, and my eyes consumed the beauty the universe had laid before me, my senses returned. Even though my mind still swam from the sweet rum buzz, I felt that I was perceiving things more clearly, and with more of a sense of honest interconnectedness, than I had in all the previous years of my life. This was exactly where I was supposed to be and this was exactly the person I was meant to share it with.

This sight, this awesome display of Mother Nature's power, seemed to me to have been created specifically for the moment when Chuck and I looked up to see the moon win its war against the clouds, combine its glowing light with the tears of the gods, and shower them both down upon us. I found myself thinking that I was just a speck in relation to the vastness that is our world and all it had provided me -- and I was a hopelessly discombobulated one at that. Yet I also felt that I was precisely who I was meant to be and if the universe thought me worthy of such an awesome display as the one I was witnessing, then I must have some inherent value.

Psychologists call this a "transpersonal experience," but I call it heaven. I felt disconnected from the everyday "real" world more than I could have achieved through any amount of drugs, but more connected to who I really am -- as part of the universe -- than I would ever have believed achievable. It seemed to me that the trees before me breathed, that the water flowed through me as well as around me, and that the air caressed the grass that lined the hot springs, inspiring it to dance.

And I danced, too. My swaying was slow yet fluid; as I shifted underneath the warmth of the water, it felt like the movements tickled my soul. I remembered that Chuck had said something that I couldn't recollect verbatim, about finding "the way" or the natural flow of energy. A seed he planted during one of our many cigarette breaks was now sprouting new growth inside me. I felt that my world would change, my beliefs would change -- I was about to change.

No words were needed and we didn't speak for a while. Then I noticed a bobbing light through the trees steadily approaching us. At first I thought it was the camp hosts coming to inform us that we were trespassing and to kick us out, so my heart skipped a beat and I hastily made my way back to the stairs where my boxers sat just outside the water. Chuck was not far behind me, and we both paused, waiting near the dock for the bouncing light to arrive. I could still feel strong, positive energy from Chuck, flowing like waves of sound traveling between us and completely enveloping me. I didn't say anything, but I silently wondered whether he could feel this energy himself -- and whether his sharing the energy was intentional.

A woman's friendly, laughing voice broke my concentration, and with it the tension I'd been feeling about getting caught trespassing. Chuck and I turned to face each other in perfect sync and it was clear that we both thought the moment somewhat comical.

I watched as Chuck pushed off from the stairs, gliding through the water just under the surface. The wavy outline of his body shifting through the dark waters as he moved further away caught my attention. As I pushed off in his direction still felling weightless and held in thoughts I had yet to fully process Chuck emerged from the water. I could see the moonlight glisten off the beads of water that streamed down his body. Like small fluorescent teardrop racers, the droplets chased each other down his pale skin, taut over his muscles. Again I wondered whether my admiration of his form was inappropriate, but regardless of my thoughts or feelings, I couldn't help but acknowledge the fact that he was an extremely good-looking man.

Chuck thought it best for us to go introduce ourselves to the new guests splashing into the springs, and so after we put on our boxers, we moved in that direction. Basically the entire south side of the swimming hole was a dock which housed the changing rooms and various sets of stairs that jut down into the waters giving multiple entry points. Chuck and I were at the last one, closest to the spring itself and subsequently the furthest from where the new visitors had made their entry. There were two men and two women in the group. The men were both shorter and heavier than Chuck and me. They were young men, and had military-style buzzed haircuts. They also wore Oakley sunglasses, which was kind of awkward given that it was...night. The women were giggly and loud, and wore two- piece swimming suits that showed off their curves well. They had long dark hair and smiles that almost illuminated the darkness around us.

"Maybe that's why the guys have sunglasses on," I whispered out loud before I could stop myself. Thankfully, I was not loud enough for anyone to hear or take notice that I had said anything at all.

Even though I remember what they looked like, I forgot each of their names as soon as they were spoken. But given the amount of booze and pot being consumed, I was pretty sure that they had done the same with me.

No matter. I was feeling great, and it seems right that the part of the conversation that had a lasting effect on me was the sheer amount of laughter that was taking place.

Before long I found myself taking hits from a joint, listening to two or maybe it was three different stories, and laughing with an ease I found liberating. One of the ladies began telling a story about why her right shoulder and neck hurt so severely. There was something about road construction, missing a sign, and barreling off into a large dip that had her catching air in her old Honda Civic. She recounted the whole thing with such a whimsical nature to her voice that it sounded like a child told the story. With another pass of the joint and a fairly decent exhale, I announced that I had experience as a massage therapist and I offered to work on her traps and delts to see if I could assist her in gaining some relief.

I had a sudden worry that one of the men in the group might think I was hitting on his woman, but the way they all suddenly became enthusiastic about the massage made the fear go away.

Was I hitting on her? I couldn't help but ask myself as I placed my hands on her warm, tanned flesh. *She certainly had a body to be admired.*

The massage instigated a barrage of questions about various aches and pains, which led into a rather lengthy discussion about how one of the men felt unable to feel rested even after sleeping. He argued every point that the other woman -- most likely his girlfriend -- was making, but he finally agreed to doing some stretches that I recommended and maybe, just possibly, going to see a sleep specialist. She smiled at me in appreciation, while cracking open another beer and passing the tightly rolled blunt back in my direction.

There was more laughter and half-completed conversations between the six of us, but I was wholly unsure exactly what we were discussing and if it really had any significance, or if I was just too high to care. Oddly enough it was during this random exchange of pointless stories and stoned antics when I came to the happy realization that I wasn't the oddball out. I actually fit in.

A little later, Chuck and I began to slowly work our way back to the warmer section of the springs where we had started. I have no distinct recollection of exactly how our conversation with the others ended, but I know it was very friendly, with hugs, handshakes, and a fond, "Have a good night."

After another full immersion in the water, I found myself rising up to gaze at the moon again. The passage of time had meant little or nothing to us over the past several hours, but now it was pushing 3:00 a.m., and we reached an unspoken agreement to call it a night and return to our tent. The tent that waited beyond the long boardwalk, through the two separate trails amongst bear sign plastered trees, and comfortably set just the other side of the Alaska Highway.

The walk back carried with it a physical heaviness, due to the late hour, the rum, marijuana, and warm water -- yet my heart felt exactly the opposite. I sometimes felt like my tired legs would cause me to me stagger rather than continue on, but somehow I managed to navigate the damp planks of the wooden path set inches above the swamp-like sulfur marshes.

"This has been one of the best nights I've had in a long time," I confessed to Chuck.

He nodded his head and mumbled something inaudible in agreement, but his body language and the tone of his voice made it clear that he too was enjoying himself. Unable to contain myself, I continued,

"I will not allow this to be the last time I get out and do things like this. I am tired of living life to work so that I can hold on to material things. I want to be out enjoying experiences and meeting people and..." I paused to search for the right words, but none seemed to present themselves.

Chuck looked over to me, made eye contact and said, "I know what you mean, and I agree you should do more and enjoy more."

Silence fell between us for a few minutes, but not the unsettling kind, just the right amount to hear the rain, and absorb the beauty of our surroundings.

Once we arrived at my REI 2+ half-dome tent, we wasted no time settling in and readying ourselves to sleep the remaining hours of darkness away. Mind you, with us being this far northwest, and it technically still being summer, the sun would be up soon -- sooner than even we were fully aware of. Chuck faded off into REM sleep much faster than I did, so he let out the first of his many different snores while I remained still.

Quietly, I peered up at the top of my tent, mentally recounting the events that had happened since first I saw this hitchhiker on the side of the highway, now sleeping peacefully next to me. It may have been 15 minutes or even an hour before my mind and soul were ready to welcome slumber. Turning just slightly in my sleeping bag to see Chuck drifting among his dreams, I inhaled deeply -- very deeply -- pulling in all the energy I could, held it in for a moment, and with my exhale, thanked the designer of all that had brought me to this time and place.

> *"What is heaven, but a place we long to see?*
> *What is the darkness, except something that we fear?*
> *Light will show its beauty, when the eyes accept to see.*
> *And then there is no darkness, so why should we fear?"*

Sleep came fast and was sound and perfect in a way I had almost forgotten it could be.

~Day 3~

"One moment in time that took my breath away.
One moment in time that seemed to stand still.
Just that moment in truth, with naught to say;
A returning of hope, a strengthening of will."

~Morning Rush~

Not fully awake but not completely asleep, I lay silent and still in my sleeping bag, my eyes focused on nothing in particular, and appreciated the morning light as it filtered through the yellow-tinted rain fly that protected us from the elements. I was not sure of the actual time, but I was not concerned with anything other than making sure I absorbed each moment that I could in my permeable state of being.

Sleepiness lingered until I heard a commotion just outside the tent. For some reason, I had no real concern or curiosity about it. With the occasional shift in his bag and quiet snore, Chuck remained asleep while I pondered the impact of the previous night's events. It had been quite liberating and inspiring, and I couldn't help but feel that I would never be quite the same again. Somehow I knew it was an authentic experience that could not be mitigated by insecure thoughts or rationalizations.

Taking a moment to look over at Chuck, I was struck by the fact that people who are sleeping have an air of innocence. There is a unique calmness in the face that shows how the day's worries and stresses fall away. As Chuck lay there unaware of what was taking place around him, I wondered what he was dreaming or feeling. He had the calm, expressionless face of a man without a single burden.

I wondered whether I appeared this calm and peaceful while I slept, and searched all the places in my soul that held memories of past hurt. I longed to push them away like a blast of wind on the fallen leaves autumn.

Returning to the present moment, I noticed Chuck's position showed his face rather clearly and his age genuinely shown through. This observation made me all the more curious as to how he had gained so much knowledge being so young.

I was interrupted in this musing by noises outside, and a shadow that was cast against the nylon of the tent. It was not a large shadow, but it was one that could not have been cast by a human, so I began to worry as to the nature of our visitor.

Typically, I would have been rather close to a panicked state, waking everyone up and trying my best to resolve whatever issue or insecurity was plaguing me. This time, however, I was able to focus with calm reserve on the situation and wait to see where it would lead.

Not two minutes had gone by when the noise stopped and the shadow shrunk out of sight, leaving me thankful that I had maintained my composure and did not wake up the peaceful man who shared my tent. Allowing for several minutes to tick by, just to be safe, I gathered my strength and resolve to step out from our shelter. What I saw was an empty parking lot, except for two older trucks parked some 15 to 20 feet away. Off in the distance under the trees was a small black bear moving further and further away from us. Realizing that he had most likely been our visitor, and certainly an inquisitive one at that, I relaxed. He was retreating to wherever it was he called home.

Suddenly, a nice hippie-type naturalist woman, who seemed to be in her late '20s, stepped from a camper attached to one of the few remaining trucks in the gravel parking area, and sung out a warm "good morning." With a bit of a chuckle, she began telling me about how she'd seen a cute bear wandering around us just a few minutes earlier. She assured me that if it had gotten too close or became too curious, she would have certainly shouted to us or done something to send it running. Her description of the visit indicated that the bear was more interested in the wood pile we were camping next to than it was in the tent itself.

I thanked her and returned to my yellow half-dome, retrieved my glasses and phone, and set out to get my body some much-needed nicotine and caffeine. Like a junky in need of his next fix, I fumbled into my car, gathered my smokes and a bottle of Coke, and as quickly as my still-awakening body would allow, lit up and drank up. I could literally feel the caffeine course through my body, like a rush of tingles spreading to the farthest reaches within me and back again. The cold blast of caffeinated wonder zapped my weariness and replaced it with energy and the urge to get moving.

Feeling as though I could not contain this newfound liveliness, I plugged into my iPhone, queued up the first song on the playlist and allowed my mind and body to travel to that plain of existence shared only by those of us who are deeply influenced by music. Then, it was as though the notes themselves took control of my limbs. I gave into the movement they instigated, and before I knew it, I was full-on dancing in the parking lot next to the Alaska Highway at 8:30 in the morning.

Laughing to myself a bit at the thought of the truckers flying by peering over to see this odd spectacle of a grown man dancing by himself, I stopped for second to finish my Coke and cigarette, and looked around to make sure our morning visitor had not returned for a repeat stopover. Unfortunately, because my attention wasn't directed at the asphalt that separated us from Liard Hot

Springs, I nearly ended my "morning rush" with a "morning grill" -- the grill of a Mac truck barreling down the highway! After the truck passed, I decided it best to carry on with my nicotine fix and dancing closer to the trees.

Half dancing and half walking, I moved up onto the small grass-covered divider, which separated the gravel parking area. Stuck in the center was an oval-shaped sign, with a small white post and a black pointed top. The words "Historic Mile 496" stood out in black against faded white paint, calling out to me to snap a picture. This mile marker, this historic spot on the Alaska Canada Highway, would now be forever etched into my memory. I knew it marked coming changes.

These are the mornings I have always longed to have, I thought. *I was free!* I felt more unshackled than I could ever remember feeling. *Was it because of last night? Was it because of the adrenaline from our morning guest?* Could it have been some variation of these things, coupled with the thrill of good music and an ice-cold Coke?

I didn't know and I didn't care. Staring up into the morning sky, headphones blasting out "7 Cities" by Solarstone, and completely overtaken by the sheer awesomeness of the moment, I felt like not even gravity could maintain its grasp on me.

Time melted away into infinity and I gave myself the freedom not to worry about its passing. Unencumbered by thoughts, in a Zen-like state of mind, I began exploring the forest at the edge of the clearing, experiencing a weightless euphoria I once thought only illegal drugs could provide. I held onto enough clarity not to forget about the black bear, but otherwise allowed whatever feeling or desire that I had to surface. The thought came to me with clarity: *I was at one with all that I was, and all that was around me.*

"Wow that really sounds fucking lame, Drue!" I chided myself, speaking loudly enough to hear my own voice above the music filtering in through my headphones. "Where the hell are you coming up with this new age namby-pamby bullshit that you used to laugh at?"

I searched myself for answers that seemed to be right in front of me and yet somehow still remained so very elusive. But then a shift occurred. I may have sounded all new-age hippie crazy, but if so it was only because I had a radically new perspective, still in its infancy, and did not yet have the words to accurately describe it.

This revelation brought me to joyful tears and I felt a sense of a security that permitted me to continue feeling the high I had been soaking in for the past two hours. The warm sun broke free from the many clouds and through a clearing in the towering trees I caught sight of a singularly spectacular scene: a mountain reaching up to the heavens in the way only rugged peaks can.

I was held, mesmerized. Suspended in a frozen moment of time, I rested my gaze on this perfect culmination of clouds, blue sky, and mountainous rocks with a reverence for all that had been or would be created.

I am part of this. I am a part of all of this, I thought to myself, thankful to be experiencing what felt like yet another life-altering epiphany on this journey from Alaska to Florida.

Before my thoughts and the passage of time could collide like inbound trains on the same track, I woke myself from my reverie, and walked back to the tent where Chuck still slept. To my surprise, our neighborhood black bear had returned for a second morning visit. He caught sight of my movement as I cleared the trees into the open area, and dashed off in the opposite direction without a single glance back. I guessed that he would most likely give up on the wood pile until after we left, and focused my attention on waking Chuck so we could go to the springs one more time before hitting the road.

Just as I had the morning before, I stumbled on my words, wondering how I should wake this peaceful, resting soul I had grown to respect so much. Finally, as I had before, I simply called out his name.

~A Return~

Once we had everything packed up in its appropriate place, Chuck and I walked back across the street and into the recreation area where we had so bravely wandered the night before. Since we had to pay this time around, Chuck pulled out his wallet, kindly covering the cost for both of us. Although I expected the whole scene to be different when exposed to the sun (and with far less alcohol involved), the boardwalk still felt never-ending. I took mental note of each spot along the way where I had felt fearful, and giggled internally at my own silliness. We walked at a much more leisurely pace than we had the night before, giving us a chance to talk and contextualize many of the things we had already discussed during the trip: age, fear, history, sex, marriage.

"I don't want to be that old man hanging out with all the young kids, acting so much younger than his actual age that people stare," I proclaimed as we ventured around the first curve in the boardwalk.

"What do you mean?" Chuck asked. I knew that he understood what I was talking about, but that for some reason, he wanted me to elaborate further.

"Like raves. Perfect example. I love going to raves and dancing the night away, but for the most part they are filled with 18 to 24-year-olds. I'm having fun but I can't help but think what the hell is a 39-year-old doing here?" I know my voice must have sounded as awkward as the feeling I was trying to convey.

"Ok, well, you don't look like you're 39; you are fun, vibrant, and social, and you enjoy dancing. So I don't see what the problem is. Now if you were out there at 65, that might be a different story, "he said, with an emphasis that signaled to me that he not only wanted me to hear but also to accept his words.

I realized that I did. On this journey, I had discovered that I wasn't nearly as abnormal as my self-deprecating mindset had led me to believe. In years past, I had had thousands of dollars' worth of counseling, and countless other friends had said the same kind of things to me, but with Chuck, for the first time I actually believed them.

Ahead of us, the changing rooms and the springs came into sight. Because we had taken the time on the walk over to say many of the things that had been unsaid, we entered the hot waters much lighter than when we started -- or at least I did. I coasted off from the steps furthest from the changing rooms, into warmer waters than most of the people there dared to go, and I looked back up to the trees that formed the backdrop for my personal revelations 10 hours earlier. I remembered how they had instilled in me the resolve to make changes in my life. I did not want my everyday life to be consumed with work, sleep, debt, and more work. I wanted to experience more of what life had to offer. I wanted to be more like Chuck, or at least how I saw him, and less like Drue.

This is not to say that I longed to change the core of who I was, but that I wanted to fight the tendency to revert back to old habits of mind that would leave me sorrowful or feeling an unrelenting dissatisfaction with life. I had always been capable of unabashed love and compassion, and could be filled with empathy and emotion to the point of overflow, yet I also felt like I had been stuck in a vicious circle of work to live and live to work.

A new balance must be struck, I decided. The balance I saw in Chuck was what I wanted to adopt in my own life -- to enjoy the time given to me, while simultaneously making it a point to be generous with the time that I give to others. I placed my feet flat on the bottom of the springs and stood up to address Chuck, who was sitting on one of the benches that lay just beneath the surface of the water, and smiled.

"This feels really great. I am glad we decided to come again this morning," I said, my happiness readily apparent on my face.

Chuck nodded his head, "Me too."

Soon I started to feel hungry, so I asked Chuck if he felt the same way. He did, so we decided the time had come to leave these warm, welcoming waters and check out the diner just a block up from the park entrance. When I rose up from the springs and headed to the changing area, I almost felt as though I was leaving a lover behind, with each step taking me further from its warm embrace. I turned and looked back, and like a man making a promise to his wife before heading off for a long journey, I said under my breath, "I will be back."

I said it louder than I thought I did, because Chuck turned towards me and seconded the sentiment. In the changing area, as I shed my shorts and toweled off, I could still feel the effects of the warm water that had raised my body temperature.

"Did we bring the cigarettes?" I asked, pivoting slightly away from the wall towards Chuck.

Nodding, he tossed over the Canadian-brand cigarettes that would now have to take the place of my beloved Marlboros -- and there it was again, his naked form. Much as I had observed the night before, his body structure was a form to be appreciated in its evident strength. My eyes did not loiter in his direction for any significant amount of time, but I looked long enough to confirm that I was still very comfortable in his presence, regardless of how naked one or the both of us might be. Not to mention my contemplations were more intent on lighting up my Players cigarette and enjoying the opportunistic effects of nicotine on warm malleable muscles, than it was on anything—thought or otherwise—actually transpiring.

"I do hope we can order some breakfast," I said, after we had finished getting dressed and walked back to my car.

Chuck smiled and walked over to the other side of Cora, and then seconds after I unlocked the doors, dipped down into the passenger seat. My hunger, once only a nagging pull at my stomach, had become a full-fledged growl, and I wanted real breakfast food even more than I had the day before. *Oh yeah,* I thought, *and an ice-cold Coke would be really fucking great, too.*

Unfortunately the only craving I got to satisfy was for Coca-Cola. It looked like only hamburgers and French fries were on the menu, and they would have to do.

~Back on the Highway~

As we left the dinner and drove past the Liard Park entrance, I turned Cora and my attention back to the highway that lay ahead. My thoughts lingered on the miracle of one evening changing many years of thinking and understanding, and my heart longed to stay forever in the glow of the moon that shone on us the night before. That I was deep in thought must have shown on my face, because after a few minutes of silence, Chuck, half-looking at me and half peering out at the road in front of us, asked, "What are you thinking about?"

"How awesome last night was. It's really hard for me to explain, but I have to say it was one of the best experiences I have ever had," I said, attempting to express myself without sounding too much like an over-eager child, yet still wanting him to know how great I felt..

"It was pretty great, huh? I really love hot springs," Chuck said, smiling and turning his attention back to the road passing by outside his window.

I knew he was fully aware of how affected I was by all that had transpired, and he was allowing me to bask in my memories with deep appreciation swelling in my heart. We had started the new day with a feeling of connection, and I was sure it would lead us to deeper exchanges as the miles passed.

There was more sun shining down upon us today than there had been in all the previous days put together, and I found that a small part of me actually missed the rain. There was something cleansing about the showers we had experienced thus far on the trip. It was as though they had been my baptism into a new life I had only dreamed could be possible. The blue sky mixed with dark clouds, and the repeated cycles of wet and dry, had marked for me the purging of old thoughts and beliefs, and the making way for new ways of thinking.

I wondered if all of this intensity of emotion was due simply to the stresses of travel, mixed with my hypersensitive state of mind. I wasn't sure, but my emotions were running so high, I felt like I was on the verge of heartache or inspiration for hours after we left Liard.

As we drove, I marveled at the beauty around us. I caught sight of inviting, cool blue waters rushing southward from a glacier hidden somewhere in the mountains. I knew this water was fed by the remnants of our last ice age due to its color -- the tell-tale milky gray of rivers and lakes created by ice in the crevasses of the rugged Canadian Rockies. Even though I knew the water would be beyond cold, the desire stirred in me to go swimming. It turned out that Chuck felt equally drawn to the river, so without hesitation I turned into the next available pullout. It was close enough to the banks of the river that we could walk down to it.

Clearly this was another good opportunity to spark up a smoke, so with towel in hand, a cigarette burning, and an unwavering determination to enter the fast waters; I walked over to the five-foot drop off, with Chuck following just a couple feet behind.

Just imagining the cool blast of icy waters enveloping my body in the bright warm sun sparked a child-like excitement I could barely contain. Listening to the rapid flowing river cut its way through the rocks and fallen trees; I paused and inhaled deeply, as if to draw the energy from the waters into myself. This pause allowed Chuck to beat me into the water, and I could tell by his expression that it was much colder than our imaginations had led us to believe. I acted as though I did not see the cold shock sent quivering up his body, and stepped in with no regard for where or how deep. I nearly stopped breathing when I felt the sheer piercing cold of the water, and I stumbled slightly, which gave me a sudden jolt of fear. Unexpectedly, my mind flooded me with images faster than the waters which rushed around me. The whole imagined scene played out with over-saturated colors:

Somehow I overstepped the shallow bank and fell head-long into the glacier-cold river zipping by. Thrust instantly into category two rapids, I fought to regain my bearings. Chuck was near the shore watching with painful helplessness.

In my mind, I was essentially lost to the power of the rapids, yet for some reason, I felt strength well up in me. This was not a Drue who would become a victim -- not to his own ridiculously over-active thought processes, at least. I still felt like I was actually being swept away in the river, but then I mentally flipped myself over in the rushing waters and swam hard to the eddy set safely behind an out-bank. In this vision, *I* rescued me; not Chuck, not my therapist, not the pastor of my local church, not anyone else. I had found a way to believe in Drue.

I exhaled the deep breath I had taken, but imagined that I held onto the energy drawn from the winding river. *Funny, this crazy vision I saw,* I thought to myself, *Would I really be able to pull myself from these rushing cold rapids?* I felt a deeper shock of cold from the water that seconds ago could have been ice. Most likely was ice. And I pondered the fact that while in most of my frightened visions, I was a victim, in this one however, I was not. *I could and can in fact save myself,* I thought. And my fears scattered like scared rodents making a dash for the shadows when light is cast upon them. Now all I knew, felt, or could think about, was the sheer pain water this cold actually inflicts.

"Yeah, I sure as hell am not submerging my entire body into this," I stated to myself. Apparently I must have said it aloud, because Chuck quickly replied, "Me neither."

With a couple pictures taken and a new respect for the hyperborean, we decided to explore the surrounding area. The amazing contrast between the warmth of Liard Hot Springs and the cold of the river made me feel especially appreciative of the uniqueness of everything we saw.

Finally, we snapped off one more picture, of Chuck and me together next to the banks. I felt that sense of connectedness again, but it was more heightened, like a rush of emotions brought on by all that we were seeing and doing. As I walked back to the car I began to ponder, *What is taking place within me? What is happening?*

Unable to answer, I sat silent in the driver's seat, content to watch the scenery go by as I drove, and intent on calming the storm in my head before I spoke another word. I wasn't sure how many miles had past, but I was sure my stomach had turned in several ferocious circles. I wanted to talk, but I wasn't sure what to say. Then, without so much as a thought, I introduced a topic of conversation that I knew might lead us to speak about things in my past -- things that might make me feel even more vulnerable.

"So what are your thoughts on…," I began, but then halted and changed the subject, "…I really would like to hear more of your music. Would you be willing to play me a few more songs?"

Now I felt like a total ass for shutting myself down instead of sharing, since I knew Chuck was the right person to let in.

"Yeah definitely. When we stop tonight I will play a few," Chuck said, willing to oblige. He sat looking at me with a slight twist to his face that showed he was aware that I had wanted to say something more.

~Concert on the Lake~

As we approached Lake Muncho, I was reminded of my previous rides down the Alaska Highway, when I was young and innocent. The lake is vast and deep: about 300 feet at the shoreline in some areas, to over 700 feet deep further out. I've even heard it said before; there are places no depth could be found. Surrounded by towering mountains, the lake itself is a sight to rival any beautiful picture ever taken. Immense in all it has to offer visually, there are rugged cliffs made by the blasting away of earth to accommodate the road, the one on which we traveled, and green tree lined mountains flowing down to the water's edge on the far other side. A truly expansive blue lake; one that even as a child I remembered vividly. This Canadian wonder invited me to immerse myself in the tranquility of its thick azure embrace. As if that were not awe-inspiring enough, the sky had orchestrated a symphony of clouds and incoming rain that made my heart swell with appreciation. In my mind, I was only 7 years old again, and I could clearly see out the back of our '75 Ford pickup as we traveled this narrow stretch of road winding just inches away from the water. On that trip, fear had briefly overpowered me. My young mind was filled with horror stories of running off the road into the depths of the dark blue cold lake. It had been November and with the snow falling hard and fast, I had nervously watched the headlights of a large vehicle come up fast from behind. I knew with all the reasoning my juvenile brain could muster that those headlights were that of some evil snow monster with glowing eyes, hell bent on seeing us to the bottom of the lake. It seemed to approach much faster than we were traveling, and I could see sparks flying out from under its hideous body. I swore I could hear the truck growling curses at us as it gained ground. My father slowed our truck for reasons I could not imagine, bringing on a panic attack. Suddenly my breathing was labored and a sweat began to form on my brow. I tried to hide my fear from my older sister, knowing it would only increase her ridicule of me. I hardened my gaze out the back window and began praying. Then the truck -- a snow truck -- made a loud scrape and blurry flash as it suddenly drove past our green pickup, which my father had all but brought to a complete stop. Sudden relief fell over me.

Now, as I connected this memory with our position on the road, I looked out to the yellow lines broken by years of damage, and I swore I could pinpoint the exact spot where it all happened, some 30 years ago. I almost felt the need to explain all of this to Chuck, but instead I stole a quick glance in his direction and then commented on the stunning beauty that surrounded us.

Before long, I felt the urge to pull over, look back across this immense body of water, and enjoy a cigarette while watching the rain clouds roll in. I decided to stop at the far end of the lake, which was now only a few kilometers away. With a bit of a rough exit from the road onto the broken rocks and gravel of the "beach," I brought Cora to a stop, got out and lit up. Chuck followed, and to my surprise removed his guitar from the back of the car to perform an impromptu concert.

As I inhaled my Canadian smokes, I searched for reasons why cigarettes were playing such an important part in my life on this journey. I really wasn't sure; especially since they cost over fifteen dollars in Canada, but somehow the reason seemed unimportant to me as it overwhelming appeared that the lighting of rolled tobacco had become the key that opened my consciousness further and allowed other ideas and beliefs to enter.

Gazing at the lake but listening to him, I couldn't help but focus intently on the unbelievable sound emanating from this young man's vocal chords. I felt that his voice, like his wisdom, transcended his age. He started off his set with a song entitled, "Fuck You, I Love You," and I could hear how powerfully he was affected by the memory that had inspired the song. After he finished, he told me about a time when a woman he had strong feelings for rode off on a bus, staring out the back window at him. He, with a broken heart and a stiff middle finger, turned his back. As I stood there looking out to the black clouds that were slowly overtaking the blue sky, I felt that the emotion in his voice broke my heart and yet healed its wounds at the same time.

Droplets of water fell on me and a bit of a wind picked up, carrying colder air off the water, as if to dare me to remain where I was. In defiance, I held my ground, and so did Chuck, and again I felt the power of his emotions resonating in my soul. Turning from the lake to face him, I noticed that the water and incoming rain clouds were reflected in his sunglasses. I was unable to take my eyes from his face as I absorbed the raw power and feeling that he infused to his music, while watching in his sunglasses the beautiful, subtle movements of the clouds behind me.

I couldn't help but think: *Was this coincidence, or fate? Was I meant to be here and see this, feel this, live this? Had every minute of the days gone by simply been leading me here? Did it all happen just because I decided to leave Anchorage on the 15th of August at 1:30 in afternoon?*

Never one to allow a good moment to pass without questions, I berated myself on the possibilities of having more than one life affirming moment in so close a time as had occurred. But then I stopped myself from over-thinking. *Was I determined to fuck up a moment that was so clearly meant to be enjoyed? Emphatically, no!*

Releasing all questions and concerns, I focused on remaining open and still, physically and mentally and thought, *Thank you, universe.*

The rain soon made it too hard for us to remain standing out on the rocks, so Chuck and I returned to the car and settled ourselves in for another long tour, in the hope of reaching Dawson Creek that night. I wished I could say something profound, something comparable to the depth and intensity of the music that he had just shared with me. Instead I sat dumbfounded, but in a mood of complete appreciation. As music pumped out of the speakers, we used words sparingly, simply watching the world as it sped by the windows. I felt a passion swelling in me that I'd thought only other people could experience. I swore to myself and to any god that might be listening to my heart that if I could pause time and hold onto these past few days with Chuck forever, I would willingly give up whatever remaining years I still had left. But I knew that was impossible, and instead began to think about how I might be able to integrate all my new feelings and beliefs into my life once the trip was over. I reluctantly accepted that I would have to cross the Florida line and return to work and a more structured lifestyle, and then turned my thoughts to topics that were less likely to make me upset.

Interrupting my internal discourse, Chuck suddenly asked if I wouldn't mind allowing him to drive a little before we arrived in Dawson Creek. I rarely let anyone take the wheel of my little blue beauty unless I have consumed a few too many Captain and 7's, but oddly enough I felt inclined to allow him this opportunity. I saw the earnestness in his eyes as he explained that he was a safe driver, and it dissolved the discomfort I had in giving up my keys. Agreeing to switch pilot and co-pilot after our next cigarette break, we both returned to our own thoughts. My heart, somehow completely disconnected from my mind, started beating faster at the thought of how I might feel sitting in the passenger seat. With a hearty inhale, I calmed myself by focusing on the road and giving myself a simple math problem: calculating the average cost of each cigarette I burned. The coming cigarette break, the one I looked forward to with equal parts anticipation and trepidation, would mark a relinquishing of the driver's seat and might create a new dynamic in our conversations -- a thought that made me nervous. As I wrestled those thoughts down, my brain came up with the answer to my math problem: fifty-nine cents per cigarette, or roughly 11.8 cents for each inhale. It seemed a small price to pay for the magic each one had seemed to offer me on this trip -- somehow keeping me open and willing to share.

~Learning More~

What is the distance between points in my life when I have æded control and allowed monumental change to occur? How did this average guy, lost in pain, scared more often than intrigued, come to find himself sitting in the passenger seat of his own car -- allowing a man he'd only just met to drive? How was it that I willingly came to share the darker corners of my life with someone so much younger than me?

That is what I was thinking as I read some of my poems and other writings to Chuck as he drove us to Dawson Creek. One of these poems was "Muddle," and the end of it reads, "Truth unclear, undone mirror, good and evil vie./ Confuse the thought, always caught, never an answer why./ Choke one's self, looking for help, confounded blurry state./ Outside lives, insides dead, confuse and obfuscate."

I read the poem to him because I was curious to see what his reaction might be. I had no reason to believe he would judge me or think me odd, but those feelings -- so common in my life -- still threatened, due to my fragile self-confidence.

"So you believe you have to lie and hide who you are, so much so that you feel it's a requirement in your life, but it always leaves you feeling alone or left out of what everyone else is experiencing?" Chuck asked, almost as though he was stating the thought rather than asking.

"Everyone feels like they have to hide who they are once in a while," he continued. "That doesn't make you a liar or anything evil, it just means you are normal and are experiencing normal thoughts and fears others deal with too."

His words reverberated in my mind. They felt like the shockwaves of an earthquake reducing a concrete structure to rubble, the vibrations tearing down walls I thought a nuclear missile could not penetrate.

I was halfway through reading a short story I had written when I realized that with each word I spoke, I felt less and less shame and guilt. Even though some of what I read brought me to tears, I was opening a pathway to truly living and to a greater sense of peacefulness. Chuck readily interjected his opinions and asked deeper questions, fostering the atmosphere of intimacy. I was physically shaking from my reserved desire to open doors on subjects I had never breached with another person -- except maybe my therapist. Hesitantly, and in a low voice, I allowed my demons to surface.

Suicide was a theme in much of the poetry and stories I was reading, and the subject wore heavy on my soul. Yet despite the darkness of the subject, Chuck's energy remained light, energetic, welcoming, and caring. Sharing ideas of right and wrong, appropriate and inappropriate behaviors and desires held within the male psyche, we delved deeper into our own beliefs almost in time with the kilometers that sped by. With a deep sigh, I told Chuck about how I had struggled most of my life with intimacy issues. These issues related primarily to men and male friendships, and had caused a deep ache of sadness at my core. I stopped reading, stowed my laptop and shifted my position in the seat, readying myself for our conversation to explore deeper chasms within me. I knew I could stop at any time. I also knew, with equal certainty that I needed to continue.

"So is it inappropriate for a man to long for closeness with another man?" I barely got the full question from my lips when the sky began dropping pea-sized hail, like frozen teardrops from the angels watching us from above.

"What the hell!?" I exclaimed as I watched the small white pellets bounce off the hood of my car and crash against the windshield. They danced on the wet gravel highway, then scattered into slivers, bouncing back up into the sky. Each second seemed to fill the firmament with a thousand more. Then, just as quickly as they had started pelting down upon us, the frozen rain ceased, revealing a perfectly blue sky.

Chuck and I sat quietly for a few minutes in a mild state of wonder, and then, as though nothing had happened, we stepped back to our conversation.

"I think that men can be close. I don't think it's wrong or abnormal. In many other cultures it is nothing to see men hug each other as friends," Chuck said, then paused and asked, "Are you gay?"

His question burned me internally, and it felt as though my world was on fire. "No!" I answered, trying not to show the anger -- or maybe it was hurt -- that swelled up in me.

"It's okay if you are," he said calmly. His words were barely audible to me, because I felt the sourest of feelings churn in my stomach.

"Do I look gay?" I asked abruptly, allowing some of my hurt to show.

"When I first saw you; yes, I thought you were gay. Why? Is that a problem?" Chuck asked, his voice losing none of his tone of care and concern despite the fact that my voice was raised.

"I have been accused of being gay almost my whole life, and I don't like the fact that just because I am not as masculine as the average guy, that people automatically assume I'm gay," I said, with my voice growing slightly softer.

Chuck's posture changed slightly as well. He was not closed off like I thought he would be. I had had the thought and truly believed that he was going to suddenly stop the car, get out, and be rid of ridding with this insecure man that started showing his underlying fears and pains.

"It wasn't an assumption about your masculinity at all," said Chuck calmly. "I met you and I thought, 'Here is this guy who obviously has it together and he seems pretty cool, and he happens to be gay.' That was it."

Something about his subdued gestures at the steering wheel reminded me of American Sign Language. Chuck didn't know ASL, but there was a click I felt in his movement that made me feel calmer. I opened my mind further to listen without bias to what he was saying.

Chuck told me that he believed that men can and should share an intimacy rarely seen in our homophobic society.

"In our society, many of us have been raised to believe that this kind of intimacy is negative. That's been the prevalent way of thinking for many years, but it's changing. We still have a long way to go, but closeness between men is definitely seen as more acceptable today than it was 15 years ago," he explained. His body posture conveyed caring and concern.

"I had an experience with this guy that I was really close friends with for many years. Suddenly, on Facebook, he left me this terrible message about how I had somehow abandoned him when he needed a friend and then basically never spoke to me again. After a couple years passed and we were both in college, I ran into him at a friend's party and we started talking. Through our conversation, I learned that he had actually had a crush on me. He couldn't be around me at the time without causing himself a significant amount of pain, so he just broke off the connection with me to preserve his own feelings. Well, later that night, 'cause we were all drinking, we crashed at my friends place. He and I were alone in a room and he rolled over to kiss me."

I expected him to say that he pushed this guy away and left the house, letting his friend down as politely as possible. But he didn't.

"I leaned into him and basically we kissed," said Chuck, completely surprising me.

As he told the story, he conveyed to me strongly that my craving to be close to other men was not only acceptable, it was also not all that unusual. I was curious to explore further how he was thinking, not about homosexuality per se, but about wanting to be close to and relate to another male.

"So kissing another man doesn't make you gay?" I asked, my voice breaking under the stress of the emotions that pushed against my throat.

"Not necessarily. Just because you want to be close to another guy and share platonic intimacy, it doesn't make you gay. If you prefer men to women, then yes, you would be gay," said Chuck without hesitation.

"I've only ever thought I wanted to be with women, but I do have a strong desire to be close to men," I said, surprising myself with my confession. "Not all men, but..." I stopped, unable to finish the sentence. All at once, I felt a combination of anger, hurt, confusion, fear, and I wondered, yet again, *Who was Drue?*

The truth was that I had suffered sexual trauma at the hands of an aggressive male. After that experience, I had struggled with the concept of being close to or even sharing limited quarters with other men. I kept this fear hidden; letting it mold one of the many masks I wore daily to protect myself. The real me surfaced only when I was in therapy...or drunk.

Now I felt like I was on the verge of telling this man, whom I'd only recently met, secrets that I had been hiding not only from others, but clearly from myself as well.

I had always hated the idea of talking about homosexuality and whether it did or did not apply to my life. But that hatred seemed to stem from fear, and in this conversation, my fear was going away. I truly wanted answers, and I thought maybe I could find some, with Chuck's help.

I told him about my past experiences, and Chuck responded by sharing his innermost feelings. I knew that Chuck could and did understand me. As we talked, I felt a shift inside me, a shift that I never would have recognized unless I had become fully aware of my own hurt: I was beginning to accept myself. For what seemed like the first time in my whole life, I didn't feel an uncontrollable desire to berate myself or belittle who I was.

Up until that point in my life, it had been normal for me to fantasize about having a different past, a different life. *If only I wasn't so lonely. If only I wasn't so disabled by my fear. If only…*

"Holy shit!" said Chuck, snapping me back to reality. His hands gripped the steering wheel with white-knuckle intensity, and I looked up to see the road covered across both lanes with a blanket of snow. Chuck applied a bit more pressure to the brakes than I felt altogether comfortable with, and continued to verbalize a bunch of words which to me sounded like the same word. "Shit!"

Time seemed to stand still as we drove onto white snow, with no tire tracks or any other indication of anyone having traveled there before us. I was struck by the fear that we were going to start spinning out. It seemed as though all of life was contained in these two tenths of a mile that we were in the midst of traveling. It felt all the more strange because snow rarely blanketed the ground this far from the mountain tops in summer, even in the late summer.

Then the stretch of white snow ended as abruptly as it started, and we looked at each other with equal parts confusion and appreciation for the absolute oddity of what we had just experienced. I believe at least two exclamations of "What the hell?" escaped our mouths before we regained our normal speed and Chuck set Cora back on cruise control.

By then it wasn't far from dusk and I knew there were many more kilometers ahead of us, but I was in need of nicotine and a stretch, so I asked that we stop, and Chuck, with a cute boyish grin, agreed.

Wow! Cigarettes taste good when your nerves are rattled and your heart is racing, I thought to myself as I gazed up into the darkening sky, inhaling a larger than normal hit on my cig. *This certainly has been a trip of odd occurrences and awesome advances.* Irrevocably smoking would be connected to this trip; to these advances in perception. I was being changed and my small white cylinders of tobacco—Canadian or otherwise—had some part to play in it. I mused about whether cigarettes were somehow the local anesthetic that allowed me to handle all of this deep exploration of the aching sores that spotted my soul. I wasn't sure, but regardless, I was grateful. With a slight downward glance, I pressed my foot into the gravel, the cigarette was gone, and the moment was over. The feelings, however, lingered in me like the smoke still swirling within my lungs.

~Healing~

*O*ur arrival in Fort St. John came with the realization that we should stay there for the night, considering that we both were hungry and would like a beer, or two, or twelve. Fortunately, our hunt for a cheap hotel paid off rather quickly, as we saw a small, older place right next to the highway. Simple but clean, the hotel had that unmistakable smell that all inexpensive hotels have, mixed with the faintest scent of marijuana that I caught wind of in the hallway as we walked to our room.

The room had the typical off-white walls and early 90's décor, and it hummed with the sound of a window A/C unit that was louder than the traffic just a few hundred feet away. With two full size beds, a TV, shower, and small fridge, it had everything we needed for our last hours of traveling together.

I was eager to relax in a warm shower and throw back a few beers, so I didn't hesitate to unpack just enough to achieve said goal and made a quick but respectful exit to the bathroom. Meanwhile, Chuck enjoyed some much-missed television. The water rushed over my body, and although it smelled rather strongly of chlorine -- as the water does in most hotels -- I enjoyed the sensation. It felt as though I could see the exhaustion from the day's drive simply wash off me with each drop jetting from the oversized shower head.

I was wishing I could've partaken in the marijuana that brought the fragrant aroma of THC into the hallway, but in a way my memories of the last few days were just as much of a high. But as I started to relax, I felt a mixture of hopes and fears blast their way into my consciousness, like dynamite on the side of a mountain, as though the goal was to clear everything away in preparation for a massive rebuilding. Something in me was fighting for the chance to lay a new foundation of beliefs and understandings. It was not an altogether unpleasant feeling, but it certainly kept my nerves on edge. I tried to rid my head of all thoughts except how good the hot water felt running down my body. Then, faintly, I heard Chuck laugh, presumably at something on the TV, and I managed to gather my thoughts into one simple idea: I wished I could remain on the same path as this once-stranger, now friend. I longed for a way to postpone my arrival in Florida and simply continue on with Chuck to Seattle. But the realist in me knew this was impossible.

I took one last minute to allow the shower to wash away these thoughts and desires, and then shut the faucet off with a bit of a metallic clank. When I was dry and clothed, I headed straight for the beer that Chuck had so generously purchased for us. Only three years before, you wouldn't have caught me drinking a beer unless it pertained to some sort of dare. Yet since I had moved to Alaska, I had gradually grown a taste for the hoppy beverage. Now I looked forward to knocking back a few brews while eating my favorite Wendy's chicken sandwich and watching some obnoxious cartoon on Adult Swim. Chuck was already a full beer ahead.

In fact, many things had changed in my life since moving to Alaska, and it looked like they would be changing again as I was making my way from the Great White North to the Sunshine State. It seemed it was a true journey of discovery; these three days on the highway accompanied by such and open spirit. His transparency had in turn opened my soul up to the possibilities of new paths. A gift from the universe which answered so many prayers I had once blindly voiced to the heavens. It was the catalyst to a revolution in my understanding. Inspired by these thoughts, I decided to show Chuck some of the sign language videos I had made. He and I sat on the bed, watching videos on my laptop while enjoying the second of our Left Hand Brewing Co. beers.

"You're a good actor," Chuck said after watching my video translating "Coming Undone" into ASL. He told me in a complimentary tone of voice how well I played the role of someone close to insanity. It was clear that he hadn't meant it as an insult, but as a kind, gentle jest. Still, I wondered if I was truly acting in that video, or if I really was someone who had little control of his sanity—*mind bent and losing it*—but hid it well. Was the real Drue the one I showed to people in everyday life -- or the part of me that often lay panic-stricken at night, in tears, wishing I could share myself with someone who would willingly accept who I was? Tonight, I believed I was both.

I am both the man I present, and the man who struggles with wanting to be accepted and held safe, I told myself.

Dismissing these thoughts, I reminded Chuck that he had promised me a mini-concert of his original music when we arrived at our hotel. As he readied his guitar, I stretched myself out on the firm mattress, with a pillow tucked under my chin, my happy anticipation showing in my smile. As Chuck tuned his guitar, a six-string classic wood instrument, I felt like I could almost see his energy freely flowing out from his being, like waves of liquid fire. It was flickering and dancing, flowing outward and consuming everything around him. Strumming his guitar a couple times and readying himself, Chuck looked over to me and with a shift in the right corner of his lips, and closed his eyes.

He began with *Clown* because he knew it was my favorite, and I felt myself caught up in his energy, and fed it with my own. I could hear in these songs the pain of a man who was wiser than his years, yet whose heartache was still fresh and young. Meanwhile, like a tiger tearing its way through the flesh of a fresh kill, my own doubts and fears battled with my newfound confidence and self-acceptance. Sometimes, it felt like his lyrics had been specifically written to address something I felt or needed to feel. Painful memories surfaced, and I could not control how weak they made me feel just below the surface of my smile. I almost *wanted* to cry, because crying might cleanse me of the pain that was crippling me and robbing me of confidence.

After Chuck played his last song, there was a silence for what I am sure was only a second or two. But in those moments I felt acutely aware of the emotional atmosphere between us. I was letting go of my inner turmoil. I thanked Chuck for his songs as he packed up his guitar and made a polite exit to the restroom.

While Chuck enjoyed a warm shower I continued drinking my dark red lager. Liquid courage or a barrier solvent, it spread its numbing effects through my body like a shot of Novocain. It was like I was purposely deadening the nerves of a tooth to be pulled. And like a stubborn tooth in the gums, my fears seemed to lodge themselves more deeply in my soul.

With all the mental power I had left in my buzzing mind, I tried to convince myself to hold back from exposing more of my feelings to Chuck, but I couldn't help myself. Fresh from the shower he was now lying comfortably in his bed, watching the TV while polishing off another beer, and looked over to me as I stumbled on the words to get his attention. *Stop Drue, you do not want to do this*, I told myself, willing myself to keep my mouth shut.

Chuck simply looked over at me with an expression of deep understanding, as though he already knew the question I wanted to ask but was patiently waiting for me to say it. I made a last-ditch effort to come up with a question unrelated to what I really wanted to ask. "Do you mind...," I began, then stopped as Chuck dropped his head in a welcoming shift to the side. Something in me interpreted this gesture as an invitation to speak truthfully, so once again I pushed words from my throat, "I was wondering if I...?" Before I could even finish my request, Chuck spoke, "Come over here and get in my bed."

I felt as though my consciousness dropped a thousand feet, and I noticed that my body began to sweat and my heart began to beat so rapidly that I visibly shook as I tried to move towards Chuck's bed, only three feet away.

"We can't do anything," Chuck said, and paused. "But you can come lay over here with me."

"That is all I need," I said, in a broken, squeaky voice.

As I circled the foot of his bed, I could hardly believe what was happening. A warm rush of feelings exploded in me, like fireworks lighting up a night sky. I could think clearly but my mind was racing. My chest shook with each breath that I tried consciously to slow. My ears rang and I could hear my heart pulsing in them.

These bodily reactions began to ebb slightly as I crawled under the covers that Chuck was holding up and moved in closer to his warm, welcoming embrace. With a swift but graceful movement, Chuck reached his left arm around from behind me and rested it upon my shoulder, pulling me down to his chest so that my head could lay there comfortably cradled against him.

Tears had not yet began their ascent of my eyelids, but were ever so near the verge and simply waited there for me to allow that one moment of weakness that would give them the perfect opportunity. Without warning or provocation, the lyrics to a song I had not heard for a long time began playing in my mind. It was a song by the Pet Shop Boys, but in my head it was sung more like a lullaby: "Is this real, can I learn to trust, how do I feel, does darkness end in light? Never been closer to Heaven."

I had no power, no control, and no way of stopping what was about to happen. The dam broke, all of my pain rose to the surface and came rushing out, with tears pouring from me harder than I had thought possible.

"Let it go, Drue." Chuck half whispered to me. "Soak my shirt, you're safe, just let it all out."

As though my soul had been waiting for permission to cry, I did just that. The words that Chuck so caringly whispered to me dispelled all my fears. I was safe, comfortable, held. I am fundamentally a social being who needs connection with his brothers and sisters, and right then, every fear I had had about what is right or wrong, moral or immoral, no longer had any relevance to me. The only power in that room was the bond of unconditional closeness that I was feeling to a fellow traveler in the journey of life.

Chuck stayed silent, quietly rubbing my shoulder and holding me tightly to him, not trying to fix me, not trying to solve the mystery of my pain. He just allowed me to cry in the safety of his confident embrace.

"I can hear your heart," I mumbled through my tears, barely able to speak. "Are you okay with this?" I asked, hoping that I was not making him feel uncomfortable.

"You hear my heart don't you?" he replied, and I nodded yes. "It's slow and steady, not erratic or racing. Right?" he asked. Again I nodded yes. "If this were not okay, that would not be the case. So just relax, Drue, you're safe, and everything is all right."

A sense of peacefulness blanketed me, warm next to his body. I felt that not only was this okay, but that *I* was okay. I knew some people might think that this situation was odd or even abnormal, but something in me understood that what they thought had no meaning in the face of this miracle. There was no reason that I could not experience the closeness that I had been starving for.

I felt a profound contentment that banished all of the insecurities my vivid imagination could craft. So I rested there, close to a friend, listening to his heart, remembering all the blessings that life had given me on this trip. I breathed in the energy of our connection. It felt like all the music we had shared, all the conversations we'd had, both on and off the road, had led to this moment. This moment felt as though it had been orchestrated by the universe to help me heal. The nefarious demons of my past, the manipulative creatures of my present, and the damning judges of my future -- all were vanquished. There was no war inside me, no battle for dominance, and no need for anyone to have control. I was not required to posture, fake it, or hide my emotions. I was, at last, allowed to just *be*.

~ Day 4~

"Changes and renewal, thoughts and fears;
moving towards the next stage, joy and tears."

~Breakfast Achieved~

The next morning as we readied ourselves for leaving the hotel, my heart ached to say something, but I found that I could not utter a single syllable. Somehow I was more content to share music and allow my mind, spirit, and will to accept the knowledge that Chuck would be departing soon.

"You okay?" Chuck asked, showing his natural tendency to care.

"Oh, I'm fine," I answered. And I really was.

Our drive that morning took us up and over hills and through neatly carved gorges, as we listened to an eclectic array of music and shared light conversation about the sub genres of techno and rock. As we reached the outskirts of Dawson Creek, close to highway 97 where Chuck would make his backtrack towards Seattle, we came across a small diner that appeared promising in the hope that we might get breakfast. I'm sure it had something to do with the, "We serve breakfast 24/7" marked across their front windows.

It's funny how I had been relating to breakfast on this trip. It was like a quest, as we had traveled over a thousand miles in search of the breakfast food that would satisfy our cravings. And this morning, this last morning that Chuck and I would spend together, we finally found what we were looking for. Finally, a plate of eggs, bacon, and toast -- our reward, finally achieved, and eagerly welcomed.

"I like the darker, more experimental sounds of dub step," Chuck admitted, in the middle of our breakfast conversation. It was something that I had already surmised.

"Definitely, I agree, I've always preferred the darker aspects of experimental electronic music," I said. We continued to talk throughout the meal, as we savored the end of our quest and enjoyed plates of food much larger than our stomachs could handle, but with smiles large enough to show how happy we were to try. It was the same with the celebratory smoke that we shared afterward -- both the meal and the cigarettes were full of flavor and relaxing in their effects on my nerves.

I found myself wishing that this cigarette, this Canadian-bought Camel light, would burn for hours.

"You okay with last night?" Chuck inquired.

"I feel a bit odd, but as long as you are cool with it, then I am okay," I said, struggling through the words. I didn't feel like what we did was bad or wrong, but I felt the need to be sure that Chuck didn't feel put off in any way by the night's events.

"We are good," Chuck said without any hesitation, and then continued. "You really needed that. I know you must feel a bit strange or awkward, but I want you to know, everything about last night was, and is, okay."

I could tell he was speaking from a place of genuine concern for me. Feeling as though a significant amount of weight had been lifted from my shoulders, I smiled, told him how much I had enjoyed having him in my car for the past three days, and then asked, "Can we stay in contact?" I paused for a moment, "Like on Facebook?"

"Sure," said Chuck, while pulling a business card from his wallet and handing it to me. "This is my email and phone number. If you use my full name there on the card, you should be able to find me on Facebook, no problem."

I knew that distance would separate us during our day-to-day lives, and I also understood that contact with him, physically, might never occur again. As disappointing as that was for me, I could accept it. The thought of friending him on Facebook, though, made me feel much less like I was saying goodbye and more like I was simply saying, "see you later."

~Found~

*T*here were only a few miles left between our breakfast location and the highway turnoff where Chuck and I would part ways. I peered up at the bright sun shining down on us, soaking in the warmth of its rays as I drove steadily at about 80 kilometers per hour. I didn't know how I would feel when the two of us were no longer sharing the cabin of my little blue beauty, and I almost allowed fear and doubt to worm their way back into my heart.

Thankfully, I knew that would be the worst possible thing I could do, and I turned my thoughts instead to the memories of Liard Hot Springs, lakeside camping, concerts on the shores of Lake Muncho, and the hours of conversations that had me feel such a deep sense of self-acceptance and confidence.

I had broken the shackles of my slavery, and I was becoming the man I dreamed I could be. My story was new, unwritten. *I was found.* This trip had brought me face to face with my fears, had given me a new way to think about myself, released me from the constant need to berate myself, and finally helped me understand that I was unique but normal. It had been a three-day expedition into my soul, and one which rendered three-fold rewards. Laughter edged its way up and past my lips. It wasn't loud enough to be heard over the music, or distracting enough to pull Chuck's attention away from the window, but it cemented the smile I had been wearing.

I know who I am today, I said to myself, and it felt like a secure statement of fact. I was no longer just a mask to hide behind; I was not, nor would I be again, the man I was before I left Anchorage.

Not in church, not in nightclubs, and not in therapy sessions did I figure out who I am. No...I found myself in the vast landscape of the northern hemisphere. I found myself on a highway stretched out between two countries sharing a single continent, hidden amongst glaciers and wilderness. Because I opened myself to this stranger; because I lost myself on the ALCAN, I found Drue. A single joyful tear raced down my left cheek.

I pulled off to the side of Highway 97 just about 5 miles down from the historic mile one marker in downtown Dawson Creek, hitting the flashers on Cora with a heavy heart, but an uplifted spirit.

I knew I would miss Chuck and that it would be hard, but he had given me gifts that I would have for the rest of my life, and that encouraged me. Checking, checking again, and then double-checking everything, Chuck and I

Cora for all his belongings and necessities. Once we were certain he had everything, Chuck grabbed hold of me and pulled me to him for a hearty hug and thank you for the ride. He made me feel safe, and I felt that everything that had transpired between us was natural and good. Our hug ended, and Chuck gathered up his gear. I returned to my car and readied myself for the last part of my journey to Florida. I hit the push-button start and signaled my intent to U-turn back onto the road. The blinking green arrow seemed to beat in time with my pounding heart, as I watched Chuck throw his bag over his shoulder, rest his guitar across his back and begin walking up the highway.

Although there may have been other sounds, I heard only the pulse of my heart booming in my ears as I pressed the gas and turned my car eastward. Looking back through the side mirror, I managed a hesitant smile as I watched Chuck's figure fade off into the distance.

Our time together was over, but my journey was far from ending.

The Master observes the world
but trusts his inner vision.
He allows things to come and go.
His heart is open as the sky.

tao te ching
~12~

About the Author:

Drue M. Scott was raised in many different States across America which fostered his enjoyment for being outdoors. Discovering his love for journaling and poetry at an early age, his passion for the transportive power of writing has, and still continues to, shape his life. Drue currently lives in Orlando Florida where he works as a Sign Language Interpreter while finishing a degree in Psychology.

Contact the Author:
    akdaydreamer@hotmail.com